Etsuo Miyoshi

My Polio Unlocked the Door to Sustainable Peace:

Invention, Health, Linguistic Equality

Etsuo Miyoshi

Senior Advisor, Swany Corporation

Born in 1939 in Kagawa Prefecture.
Contracted polio at the age of six months, resulting in the impairment of his right leg.
In 1964, as senior executive of Swany, began to travel abroad to develop markets for ski and cold-weather gloves.
Invented the Swany Bag, a cabin baggage-size bag based on a wheeled suitcase seen in New York, designed to support the user's weight, and the Swany Mini, the world's smallest folding wheelchair, both hit products.
He later served as President and Chairman of Swany Corporation, and now serves as a Senior Advisor.

Swany Corporation
981 Matsubara, Higashikagawa City, Kagawa Prefecture, Japan 769-2795
URL http://www.swany.co.jp
E-mail wb@swany.co.jp

The English translation is by Charles Rowe, who received his PhD in Japanese music from the School of Oriental and African Studies, University of London, in 1997. A speaker of Esperanto as well as English and Japanese, he lived in Japan for many years, during which time he studied at the Tokyo National University of Fine Arts and Music and worked at the Oomoto Foundation. He is a performer and researcher of the music of the Japanese two-stringed zither *yakumogoto*. A professional translator for 40 years, he is active in the Japanese language network of the Institute of Translation and Interpreting and is a contributor to *The New Grove Dictionary of Music and Musicians*. His other translations include *The Great Onisaburo Deguchi* by Kyotaro Deguchi and *The shakuhachi and its music* by Tsuneko Tsukitani.

Etsuo Miyoshi

My Polio Unlocked the Door to Sustainable Peace:

Invention, Health, Linguistic Equality

*Recommendations
for an active life
that turns despair
into hope*

Print and Publish: BoD – Books on Demand, Norderstedt

ISBN 978-3-7597-4908-6

**My Polio Unlocked the Door to Sustainable Peace:
Invention, Health, Linguistic Equality**

Written by: Etsuo Miyoshi
Translated by: Charles Rowe
Cover design: Hiroki Nakamitsu

Japanese edition: ASA Publishing Co., Ltd.
http://www.asa21.com

Preface

I was born in a small town in the northeast corner of the Japanese island of Shikoku, a town famous for its glove industry, and I inherited my father's glove business. In the last half century, fierce competition has brought the number of glove manufacturers down from more than two hundred to a quarter of that number. It was inevitable that a labour-intensive industry such as ours would be hit by rising labour costs, but we were saddled with a further weakness – the fact that we made a seasonal product that sells only in winter.

After succeeding to the family business, I worked hard to sell our little firm's products to the world, but breaking away from our reliance on a seasonal product was a challenge. The only way to meet this challenge was to come up with a striking new product.

After much hard effort, we developed the body-supporting Swany Bag and the world's smallest folding wheelchair, the Swany Mini.

The impetus behind this product development came from my own disability, caused by having polio just after I was born. In this book, I should like to share some of the drama involved along the way.

Later, I suffered a kidney disease, from which I recovered after undergoing difficult fasting therapy. I shall also be writing about my experience with this health regime.

Next, I shall discuss my involvement with the question of an international language.

Since I was young, I have been an active supporter of the campaign for Esperanto. I shall explain the reasons why the question of international communication is so important and consider what will happen to the world if the English language is allowed to continue its global takeover.

This is a story of rebirth, achieved with my disability as a springboard.

In later years, I came to see my misfortune as having been behind my happiness, but meanwhile, having reached the age of 81, I find attachment to my remaining life raising its head. When talking about their own life, people have a tendency to boast. Even when they are being self-effacing, talking about their failures or negative sides, people tend to boast in a 'modest' way. The story I tell in this book is probably no exception. Even so, I hope that there is something in my life experience that might be of use in some way to others who are living with disabilities like mine, or who are facing difficulties at work or at home in the Covid-19 pandemic. I shall take the plunge and try my best to recount my experiences honestly and straightforwardly.

March 2021   Etsuo Miyoshi

The author taking a walk
with a Swany Bag in each hand

In front of
Swany Headquarters

Self-portrait in oil

Swany Bag, the bag that supports the user's weight.
For everyday and travelling use

Contents

PART 4. A FUTURE WORLD LANGUAGE   149

Afterword   167

PART 1.

UNDERSTANDING SUPPORT NEEDS

1. Karma

My background

My family home is on the coast of the Seto Inland Sea in Japan. If you open the back gate, you can see the sea and the island of Shōdoshima right in front of you.

When I was at elementary school, my summers were spent playing in pools dug at the water's edge and swimming in the shallow water. Every day my brothers and I would come home from the beach and walk into the house with the sand still stuck to our bodies, to receive a telling-off from my mother. Tsuneo Naruse, who lived next door and was at junior high school, was always with us. He used to pull me by the leg into the deeper water and watch me alternately floating and sinking. But when it looked dangerous, he would push me back to the shallows. I would swim like crazy, gulping sea water, but because I knew he was there if I got into trouble, I enjoyed the thrill of flirting with danger.

Soon I found that I could swim for about four or five metres. I swam every day, and I made such progress that by the time I went up to junior high school I was swimming hundreds of metres out to sea. The clear blue sky, the jellyfish touching me as I swam close to the shore, the small fishes darting away from me, and seeing the underwater panorama where the starfish lived when I dived down, I found myself drawn in, mind and body, to this world.

In the water, my right leg, which caused me problems on dry land, gave me no difficulty at all. I would swim for hundreds of metres across the smooth water north towards Shōdoshima, and then relax my body and rest, lying on my back. The water nearly came up to my nose and mouth, but I hardly drank any. For the four or five minutes I lay there, floating on the surface in a state of blissful weightlessness, it was like paradise on earth.

I was born on 16 December 1939, just to the west of Kyōrenji Temple in Shirotori in Kagawa Prefecture on the island of Shikoku. (In 2003, Shirotori merged with the neighbouring towns of Ōchi and Hiketa to form the new city of Higashikagawa.) When I was only six months old, I developed a high fever, and after my mother took me round all the local hospitals, I was given a diagnosis of 'infantile paralysis', and my right leg remained affected.

When I was at elementary school, we used to go into the grounds of Shirotori Shrine, a Shinto shrine next to the school, to do physical exercises. It was a wide sandy area next to the sea, with lots of tall pine trees. Because I couldn't do the exercises well, the teachers made me stand apart and look after the other boys' clothes. I really hated those exercise sessions.

But even though the others beat me at everything else, there was one thing that I was better at than they were: handstands. And the strength in my arms from doing handstands and walking on my hands was to be very useful to me in later life.

Three months before I was born, on 1 September, Nazi Germany invaded Poland, starting World War II. Two years later, on 8 December 1941, the Pacific War broke out with the Japanese attack on Pearl Harbor, plunging the world into turmoil. But my childhood memories are of distress about my leg, and of the wide-open sea, the sand, and the blue sky.

The author aged eight, 1947

Narrow escape in a rickety boat

About 500 metres west of my house there was a beach with a place where you could hire a rowing boat for twenty-five yen an hour. When I was still at elementary school, a friend told me that they were getting rid of old boats, and I begged my father to buy one. 'No,' he said in a final way, 'Boats are dangerous.'

I pressed him, 'I can't win at anything on land, but in the sea I can!'

My father thought for a while, and then said, 'How much do they want for it?'

My father, who spent his whole life working, couldn't imagine what it was like owning a boat. 'You'll have trouble when there's a typhoon. You'd better not come to me about it.' The boat would be my responsibility. 'Hooray!' I shouted.

In the afternoons and during the holidays I invited my classmates over and enjoyed myself taking them out rowing. Four of us would occupy the seat for two rowers, while one sat in the back giving directions. When the island of Hitogojima came into view, we would all yell together, 'Look, there's Hitogojima!' and we would row out to this little island about three kilometres off the coast, pulling on our oars like mad, and row round the island before heading back.

But if going was easy, coming back was harder, and we had to make a tremendous effort before we finally reached the shore, rowing a ridiculous distance for children like us.

There is a south wind that blows down from the Sanuki Mountains, which form the border between Kagawa and Tokushima Prefectures, down and across the sea to Shōdoshima. One day, my classmates went out rowing with me when this south wind was blowing. With this tailwind behind us, we reached the little island of Hitogojima in practically no time. When we got there, 'white horses' were forming on the waves around the island, and we realised that there wasn't a moment to spare – we had to set off back immediately. With the boat buffeted east and west, we struggled to keep the bow pointed south, rowing for our lives. Dozens of times we were hit by powerful gusts, but we managed to keep going. We were terrified that if the boat were to capsize, we would be carried out on the waves towards Shōdoshima.

Luckily, the boat held together, and, rowing desperately, we made it back. There, on the shore, we saw my grandfather Senzō waving a big bamboo stick and yelling:

'If you try to come ashore, I'll kill you!'

The sight of my furious grandfather frightened us, but he was desperately worried about us, and this was his way of teaching us never to go out again in a southerly wind. He became instantly famous at school as 'Etsuo's scary grandpa', and my friends stopped coming to play with me for a while after that.

When I went up to senior high school, a two-metre-high sea wall was built along the shore, and now there was nowhere to keep my boat. Boating had taught me the harshness of nature and the dangers of the sea, as well as strengthening my arms. But my rowing days were now over.

The author with family next to the island Hitogojima
(2017, left to right: the author, eldest daughter Ayako,
granddaughters Akari and Saori, and Swany executive director
Yasunobu Kawakita)

My father

My father Tomio was born on 3 October 1908, in Sanbonmatsu in the town of Ōchi, the third son of Genzō and Sumi Kyōwa, who had a total of five sons and four daughters. The Kyōwa family ran a general store, selling hardware and household goods. Soon after my father was born, his mother stopped producing milk, and so he was taken to be looked after by the Miyoshi family in neighbouring Shirotori. His foster mother Yone was devoted to him, and he grew up without ever feeling that he was being treated differently on account of being a foster child.

After about a year, my father's real mother Sumi gave birth to another boy, and since she was now busy with the new child, Tomio was left with his new family in Shirotori. When he was four years old, his mother Sumi died, and since Yone had no children of her own, he was formally adopted into the Miyoshi family.

Yasuji Miyoshi, Tomio's adoptive father, loved drinking *sake* and was forever changing jobs, and the family lived in poverty. They couldn't afford rice, and every day they ate boiled barley instead. While working as a salesperson for the drug company Teikoku Seiyaku, Yasuji found himself unable to keep up with his payments to the company, and the family's possessions were seized by bailiffs. Then came two daughters, Akiko and Takako, and a son, Ryōtarō. Now numbering six, the family really struggled. Later, the family was dealt a massive blow with the loss of Ryōtarō, now the breadwinner, in the Second Sino-Japanese War at the age of 23.

There is a story about my father not joining his class's school trip, which consisted of taking the steamboat a little way down the coast to Takamatsu, the nearest big town, because he couldn't bear to ask his adoptive mother for the money, and killing the time by tagging along with the lower year's picnic instead.

On condition that they would let him attend the last two years of elementary school, which were not compulsory then, my father went to work as an apprentice at the Takeuchi soy sauce brewery. The apprentice system was very strict in those days, and my father was treated like a servant even by his master's little children.

In a further effort to escape poverty, he bought a hen and sold the eggs to earn a little money.

Overcoming hardship and meeting my mother

When he was 20 years old, the news reached the village that Tomio's adoptive father Yasuji, who had not been heard from since leaving for Hokkaido eight years previously, had died. Tomio travelled north alone, as there wasn't enough money for Yone to go with him.

The body had been given a temporary burial at a lonely snow-covered cemetery outside Hakodate. Arriving in the evening, Tomio dug up and opened the coffin to confirm the body's identity. He was surprised to see blood flowing from Yasuji's nose, even though he had been dead for ten days.

The body was cremated straight away, but by the time the ashes were returned to him, it was ten o'clock at night. It was snowing heavily, and as he had little money, he spent the night shivering in a freezing hut next to the crematorium, clutching Yasuji's ashes.

The next day, my father took the Aomori-Hakodate ferry and then the train to Tokyo Ueno Station. It was his first time in the capital, but with no money to spare he just trudged on foot to Tokyo Main Station holding Yasuji's ashes. Two days and two nights later, he finally arrived back home.

Aged 15, having finished eight years of elementary school, my father went to work for the Kanzaki glove company, a business with just eight staff in the Fukushima district of Osaka. Working from eight o'clock in the morning till ten at night, he earned a monthly salary of five yen plus meals. As the new recruit, he also had the job of cleaning the workshop. This was not a bad wage for a youth in those days (you could buy one and a half kilos of rice for ten *sen*, or one-tenth of a yen), but by the time he went to the bathhouse at the end of the day it was past midnight.

After working there for three years he became a skilled glove-maker, and he went back to Shirotori, where he started work at the Yamamoto glove factory, an enterprise employing a few dozen people, and it was there that he met his life partner, my mother Shimeko.

When he was 17, my father had attended a lecture by Onisaburo Deguchi (1871-1948), co-founder of the Oomoto religion, and he was so impressed with Onisaburo's teachings that he became an Oomoto member on the spot.

Yamamoto glove factory (1929, the author's mother
Shimeko is sixth from the right)

In 1935, when he was 27, my father, who was the leader of the Shirotori Branch of Oomoto, was suddenly taken away to the local police station and detained. State suppression of the Oomoto religion had begun for the second time. It was alleged that Onisaburo was a traitor who was attempting to usurp the imperial throne. Tomio tried to protest, summoning all the arguments he could muster, but when he was threatened with a lengthy prison sentence, he decided that for the sake of his family the safest thing to do was to bear the injustice and make an outward show of renouncing his faith. Thus, he was able to escape persecution and return home.

My mother

My mother Shimeko (1911-1998) was born on 28 August 1911 in the village of Matsubara, the second daughter of Senzō and Nobu Tani. Her elder sister had died before she was born, so she was the only child. Although they were not well off, Senzō and Nobu were devoted to their daughter and, unusually for a farming family at that time, allowed her to stay on for the last two years of elementary school after finishing her six years' compulsory education, and they also gave her lessons in traditional dance and music. After first meeting each other at the Yamamoto glove factory, my mother and father grew fond of each other, but Senzō, my grandfather, hated the fact that Tomio was an Oomoto believer. He found the idea horrifying that Tomio was a fanatical follower of this 'sinister cult', as Oomoto was portrayed, although in later years he came to be proud of his son-in-law.

Another obstacle was the question of the continuation of the Tani family line. Tomio, although adopted, was the heir of the Miyoshi family and, since the death of Ryōtarō, the only son. Shimeko had no brothers, so if she married into Tomio's family it would mean the extinction of the Tani family. Pressured by her parents, who were loath to let the family die out (as well as being suspicious of Oomoto), Shimeko reluctantly gave up her hopes of marrying Tomio and married a man from the same town, who took her name and became heir to the Tani family – a common arrangement in Japan when there are no sons in a family.

In 1931, the year of the Japanese invasion of Manchuria, when Shimeko was 20 and had given birth to her first son, Hajime, the marriage broke down. After the divorce, Shimeko's first husband went to fight in the war in China and died in battle. After I grew up, my mother told me that the father of my eldest brother was 'resting in the highest place in the military cemetery'.

As soon as he heard about the divorce, Tomio, my father, proposed to Shimeko. Moved that his feelings for her had not changed, she accepted.

Marriage and disapproval

When my parents began their married life, my father was 24 and my mother was 21. My father left the Miyoshi house with all his belongings in a suitcase and moved in with my mother in an annexe of Senzō's house. Although my grandfather accepted their marriage and my father's moving in, he still disapproved of Oomoto. When my father was taken into custody by the police, Senzō urged him to quit the religion. Even out here in the provinces, everyone was talking about the news of the 'Oomoto incident', and the impression people had of Oomoto as a uniquely menacing cult was deeply entrenched. When he went outside, people would point and say, 'He's one of them.' My grandfather's awareness of Oomoto was no different from theirs.

Added to that, this was a time when most marriages were arranged; love marriages were a rarity, and the couple found themselves the subject of a lot of unwelcome gossip.

Because of his fear of being associated with Oomoto, my grandfather wouldn't allow the marriage to be registered, and so, until the Peace Preservation Law was repealed and the new civil code was enacted after the war, their status was that of common-law couple.

In the end, the Tani family name did not die out, but was continued by my half-brother, Hajime.

After the suppression of Oomoto began, my father was so distressed at the state's persecution of his fellow believers and the destruction of Oomoto's holy places that he lost his appetite and at one time his weight went down to 39 kilos. His siblings in Sanbonmatsu, worried that he might not survive, gave him 80 yen in lieu of a funeral offering, thinking that the money would be more useful to him in life than after his death. My father used the money to go and recuperate at a hot spring in Kyushu, but he showed no sign of recovering, and so he decided to visit a psychic from Kyoto by the name of Nakao, who was staying in Takamatsu at the time. The psychic told him that the cause of the trouble was anxiety about his religious faith and instructed him to enshrine the deity of the local Shinto shrine and pray to it, treating it as the God of Oomoto. Also, since neither the Miyoshi family nor the Tani family had been entirely happy about the marriage, they should have a fresh wedding ceremony, and then things would improve. Once he had established himself, whatever he went on to do would be a success.

As instructed, my father obtained an object of worship from the Shirotori Shinto shrine and began praying to it. He also went back to the Miyoshi family home and went out again, wearing his formal kimono, to have a proper wedding. Just as the psychic had said, my father's health steadily improved, and within four months he was his old healthy self.

Assorted siblings

In 1935, the year of the suppression of Oomoto, my sister Kichiko was born, followed by a second son, Yoriaki, in 1937. Then, on 16 December 1939, I was born as the third son. Next came a fourth son, Asao, in 1942, and finally a fifth son, Haruo, in 1946.

My eldest (half-) brother, Hajime Tani, graduated early from Ōkawa Middle School (now Sanbonmatsu Senior High School) and entered Sixth Higher School in Okayama, which changed its name after the war to Okayama University. After graduating, Hajime entered the National Tax Administration Agency, serving as Head of the Kumamoto Regional Tax Administration Bureau, and later joined the consumer credit company Orient Corporation (Orico), rising to the position of Vice President. He is a recipient of the Order of the Sacred Treasure, Third Class, and lives in Kawasaki.

Kichiko and Yoriaki were always reading books and seemed to live in a different world from their younger brothers. I remember there being a big seven-volume edition of the French novel *The Thibaults* on Kichiko's bookshelf. Sadly, she died at the age of 36, and her two children Chinami and Makoto were brought up by my parents. Yoriaki, the other bookworm, went to Waseda University in Tokyo and, after graduating, he joined Tokyo Broadcasting System (TBS), working in the News Bureau as Director, Producer, Division Director and Director of Personnel. Countless times he reviewed important documents and items for publication in the media for Swany (the glove company my father founded was renamed Swany in 1972). He now lives in Machida, near Tokyo.

According to his memory, when we were children, I was the boss, and my two younger brothers were my minions!

The fourth son, Asao, also went to Waseda University, and joined Swany after graduating. He worked hard for the company, taking charge of Swany Ikeda, Swany Kōchi, Swany Tokyo Branch and Swany Korea. He also played a key role in sorting out the chaotic situation at Swany China. He retired at the age of 50 to take up farming, his long-cherished ambition, and is now enjoying a life of self-sufficiency in Susaki, Kōchi Prefecture.

Haruo, my youngest brother, joined Swany after graduating from Asia University in Tokyo and, following his success in the branding of outdoor gloves, he became independent, taking the trademark rights in lieu of retirement pay. His 'Grip Swany' products continue to enjoy popularity with outdoor enthusiasts. Sadly, he died at the early age of 42 from bone marrow cancer, but his business continues, kept going by a new generation.

It was when I left for Tokyo at the age of 20 and my brothers came to see me that I heard one of them mention that my eldest brother, Hajime, had a different father, and first learned the truth about my own family.

2. Overcoming disability

Old US military tents – Swany's base

In 1937, my father, then 29 years old, put a sign up outside the annexe of Senzō's house advertising 'Miyoshi Sewing Machines' and went into business, at first selling sewing machines, and from the following year also making fabric gloves, having converted the upstairs floor into living accommodation for the staff. During the war, my father and five associates established the firm Toa Leather, and my father took office as a director. About 150 staff were employed making headgear for aircraft crews and other military supplies.

After the war, my father saw a new business opportunity. Hearing that the US military was selling off surplus tents and thinking that the hard-wearing tent material could be made into anything, he went to Osaka to bargain for the tents and brought them back, after successfully begging the ship owner to take them on board. But the sewing people told him that the material was too tough to sew, and they couldn't do anything with it. After much experimentation, he was able to remove the waterproof coating by rubbing rice bran into it with a scrubbing brush.

My father obtained the purchasing rights for 900 tons of old tents from the government and took out a bank loan of ¥10,000,000 (about three to four hundred million in today's money). These tents were made into trousers for coal miners, and they sold like hot cakes. The demand was huge because at this time, just after Japan's defeat in the war, there was an extreme shortage of everything.

He hired about a dozen people to scrub the tents with rice bran in the garden. I don't know what they did with the wastewater. They probably let it drain out on to the road. Later, they took the work to a shallow part of the sea nearby. Once, my father returned from a business trip to find that three of the sewing girls were missing, Hisae Okada, Tomoko Hashimoto and Masae Ōnishi. He looked all round for them, and eventually found them swimming in the sea without a care in the world. 'Hurry up and get back to work!' he yelled out to them, but they called back, 'We can't come out of the water – we've got nothing on!' It's hard to imagine such a scene nowadays, but in some ways, it was a more laid-back time than today.

When I was at elementary school, the heavy-duty miner's trousers were flying off the shelves at ¥100 a pair (about ¥4,000 in today's money), and our chests of drawers were stuffed full of hundred-yen notes. When new notes were issued after the war, bank withdrawals were limited to ¥300 per month per household, and we were keeping money in cash to avoid not being able to pay for materials and other expenses.

Once, when my father was on a crowded train, his briefcase, stuffed full of new banknotes, disappeared while he was in the toilet. It must have been a surprise for the thief to see what was inside. My father also donated money to Oomoto to help pay for the rebuilding of its centres, which had all been destroyed during the state suppressions. It was the earnings from this tent material that laid the foundation for the future Swany Corporation.

The words of the psychic had come true – it seemed that now Tomio had established himself, everything he did was a success.

In 1950, under the new name 'Miyoshi Textile Industries KK' and with an increased capital of ¥1,000,000, my father returned to his main business of glove-making. He travelled to Tokyo, Nagoya, and Osaka to build up his company's customer base, worked in the factory together with my mother to set an example to the employees, and cemented his position in the local glove-making industry.

Later, in 1969, my father became Chairman of the Japan Gloves Industrial Association, an organisation with 223 affiliated companies, and in 1972, he took office as President of the Shirotori Chamber of Commerce. Later, he was to receive the Order of the Sacred Treasure, Fourth Class.

My debt to my father

My father taught me a lot.

Once, when I was at junior high school, he pulled out the nails from an old wooden crate and told me to straighten them. I took a handful of bent nails and, instead of straightening them, I threw them into the ditch and went out to play. When I came back, my father asked me about the nails. 'I straightened them all and put them in the box,' I fibbed, but then he held out a handful of unstraightened nails and demanded sternly, 'What are these, then?' My father was very strict about not wasting anything.

My job was to fill the crates with boxed gloves, nail the crates shut and bind them with rope. Although I was small, I had confidence in my strength and dexterity, and even today I can tie a rope swiftly and tightly.

When I came home from school one day my father told me to help pack the gloves in boxes.

I took the lid off a cardboard box, put the gloves inside, and replaced the lid. 'Not like that, you fool,' he scolded me. 'Put the first lid to one side and use the lid from the next box.' I realised that doing it this way doubled efficiency. Whether it was cutting, or finishing, or whatever, he drilled into us the importance of efficiency.

Occasionally, I went with my father to visit clients. He would take me to places like Osaka, Nagoya, and even Tokyo. He had a habit of saying, 'Sales go up in proportion to time spent bargaining.' Sometimes meetings with clients went on so long that we skipped lunch, which as a young boy I found tough.

We would take the Katō Line night ferry to Osaka, and by six o'clock we would be having our breakfast at a stall at the ferry terminal in Tenpōzan, after which we went to visit leather merchants in Daikokuchō. At seven o'clock we knocked on the door of the Miyamae Store, and the boss, who was still having breakfast, welcomed us in and we started our meeting. Then, at eight o'clock, we would go next door to Nakamura Leather, where we stocked up on leather, after which we went round visiting customers in the Senba district. At the end of the day, we would take the night ferry home.

My father travelled by night to places like Kōriyama, Niigata and Kanazawa, sometimes going for a whole week without staying at a hotel, as if he were trying to get into the *Guinness Book of Records*. For him, being on the road for two nights was nothing special.

My mother's blessing

There was something not quite right about the baby.

On closer inspection, its right leg was slack, and it couldn't stand. A high fever raged for days with no sign of going down. The mother, panicking, ran around to all the local doctors.

'Infantile paralysis' was the diagnosis. And there would be aftereffects.

That baby was me at the age of six months.

As an infant, I was always clinging to my mother, and after my polio I clung to her even more. My mother went to hospitals all over Shikoku and even in Osaka, with me strapped to her back. Sometimes they offered me electrotherapy, sometimes they gave me massage.

Desperate for her boy's leg to heal, my mother turned to her Oomoto faith. Until then, she had just gone along with it out of a sense of duty to my father, but with my polio as a turning point, she now devoted herself to her religion.

If I have any good qualities at all, it is entirely thanks to my mother.

She had an inner fortitude and an openness to others and would make friends with anyone. Considerate to a fault, she was the same with all my friends. And she was generous. If a visiting friend or relative expressed a liking for an object on a shelf, she would urge them to take it home with them without hesitation.

Once, she gave all the money she had to a poor person in Takamatsu and had to persuade the station staff to let her take the train back to Shirotori without a ticket. Because of her generosity, my father wouldn't let her carry his wallet, and she never asked him to.

On her monthly visits to the Oomoto centre in Kyoto, she took the slow train from Uno to save money, saying that it gave her more time to read the scriptures on the train, and she donated the money she had saved towards funding for Oomoto's activities.

My basic philosophy of life – put all your strength into achieving your goal, fix your eyes on reality, set yourself a target, ask yourself whether you are succeeding in doing these things – comes originally from my mother's influence.

My mother, who worked hard until late at night to help my father, and still found time to practise things like flower arranging and the tea ceremony to give richness and pleasure to life, was a model to me of how to live.

If you tried to deceive her, or if you betrayed her trust, she was unforgiving. She would wait patiently for you to reflect on your actions.

Whenever I have come up against a wall, it has been my mother's upright way of life that has encouraged me.

She always spoke her mind, and she could be piercing with her candid remarks, which may have offended people at times, but her openness earned her the trust of those around her.

My father never made any comment about my mother's behaviour but watched her with a smile on his face.

My parents were frugal in their day-to-day life, and never used air-conditioning in summer or central heating in winter.

Content with simplicity, they gave to good causes without any fanfare.

Oomoto

At this point I should give a simple introduction to the teachings of Oomoto.

Hidemaru Deguchi (1897-1991), the husband of the third spiritual leader, summed up Oomoto's world view as follows:

'All things in Heaven and Earth are connected and integrated. And they are all constantly in motion. However much they move, however much they change, they are still interconnected, harmonised and integrated. This intricate and delicate unity is not something that can come about by chance. There must be a great unifying will at work, and it is this great will that we call God.

'We can't see God, but we can feel God. Consider the invisible world, the invisible power. Be awake to that which creates us and gives us life.'

In 1892, Nao Deguchi (1837-1918), a woman living in Ayabe in Kyoto Prefecture, suddenly entered a trance-like state and began to utter a series of revelations. She protested to the spirit possessing her, and the spirit ordered her to write instead. 'I'm illiterate,' she protested, but the spirit replied, 'You will not be writing, I will.' Nao went on to produce 200,000 pages of writings. These writings, known as the *Ofudesaki*, became the scriptures of Oomoto, and Nao became the religion's founder.

Seven years later, Kisaburō Ueda, a young man from Kameoka, also in Kyoto Prefecture, married Nao's youngest daughter Sumiko, and later changed his name to Onisaburo Deguchi. From then on, Nao and Onisaburo worked together to spread the spirit's teachings and laid the foundations of Oomoto.

The *Ofudesaki* contains the teachings of Oomoto on subjects ranging from cosmology to society, history, politics, economics, and life itself. Onisaburo took these writings and organised them into Oomoto's scripture so that they would be easier to understand. Onisaburo had pursued spiritual studies after undergoing his own religious experience, and this helped Oomoto's theology to take shape. Ayabe became Oomoto's ritual centre, while Kameoka became the headquarters for teaching and missionary activities.

Oomoto acquired the site of Kameyama Castle in Kameoka in 1919. This castle had a long history, having been built by Akechi Mitsuhide, who attempted to become ruler of Japan in the 16th century. The religion grew rapidly in the interwar years, attracting people from the military as well as intellectuals with its doctrine of 'reconstruction', and had considerable influence as a movement for the transformation of society.

The state grew fearful of Oomoto, viewing it as a threat to the Emperor's authority and to its own religious ideology, and as challenging the warlike mood of the time with its pacifist message. In 1921 and again in 1935, the state comprehensively suppressed Oomoto, invoking the law against lèse-majesté and the repressive Peace Preservation Law. The sanctuaries on both sites were destroyed using dynamite, and the leading members were imprisoned. Thousands of believers were rounded up, and sixteen lost their lives.

With Japan's defeat in the war, the leaders were acquitted of the charges of lèse-majesté and violation of the Peace Preservation Law, and Oomoto's innocence was established. The lawyers urged Onisaburo to seek compensation from the government in the courts, but Onisaburo renounced the right to claim compensation, saying that any such payment would come at the expense of a defeated people who had already suffered enough. This also meant that many of the facts of the affair never came to light.

Under the slogan 'One God, one world, one international language', Oomoto has been active in promoting interfaith dialogue, forming partnerships with Taoists, Christians, Muslims, and others; the world federation movement, which aims at the establishment of a world government; and the popularisation of the international auxiliary language Esperanto as an easy and neutral medium of international communication.

Oomoto's aim could be summed up as the salvation of humanity through a reconstruction of the world.

My parents join Oomoto

My father visited the Oomoto headquarters when he was 17, and heard the 54-year-old co-founder Onisaburo speak for the first time. Onisaburo already had quite a reputation as a prolific poet who produced verses by the hundred, as a possessor of psychic powers, and as a dynamic activist, and was called variously a 'great prophet', a 'monster', and an 'adventurer'. However, Onisaburo had not a trace of pomposity, and my father was attracted to his common-man appeal. According to my father, when he heard Onisaburo talk about the spiritual world and the reality of eternal life he felt the presence of a great light illuminating his future and he felt filled with a spiritual power such as he had never experienced before.

My father, who had undergone hardship and humiliation, found himself shaken to his soul by Onisaburo's teaching of the transformation of a world ruled by the power of money. He became a member on the spot and resolved to live modestly without pursuing wealth and status, and to spread Oomoto's teachings.

In 1935, my father became leader of the Shirotori Branch of Oomoto, and in 1958 he took office as head of the Shirotori Regional Office. From 1964, he served as head of the Kagawa Prefectural Headquarters for 12 years, and as a member of the Oomoto Council of Deputies for 26 years.

My mother, following Oomoto's teaching that 'art is the mother of religion', practised Japanese poetry, calligraphy, painting, tea ceremony and flower arranging, and played the two-stringed zither, the *yakumogoto*. She applied herself to all these things, seemingly never feeling tired from work. She also kept a diary nearly all her life.

In 1952, she became leader of the Oomoto Shirotori Women's Association, in 1961 she became Chair of the Oomoto Kagawa Federation, and in 1965 Chair of the Oomoto Shikoku Women's Liaison Council. Outside Oomoto, she became Director of the Shirotori Centre for Working Women in 1971. In 1982, she became the first Chair of the newly reorganised Oomoto Women's Association, in which capacity she travelled all over the country delivering lectures. From 1983 to 1988 she served as a councillor on the General Council of Oomoto, and from 1986 she was Chair of the Oomoto Friends of Esperanto.

Struggle with disability

Despite my mother's desperate efforts, my polio left me with a disability in my leg.

Fortunately, I could walk unassisted, but my right leg was poorly developed and weak. A struggle with this disease had begun, a struggle that would last my whole life. And yet I believe that if I had not had this disease, neither the person that I became, nor my company, would exist.

Until I was in the lower years of elementary school, my mother Shimeko took me regularly to Osaka University Hospital. In the 1930s, the transport links were not as good as they are now. First, we had to take the Uno-Takamatsu ferry across to the mainland, and when we arrived at Uno, the passengers ran for the Okayama train, pushing and jostling each other, leaving us to follow on behind. At Okayama, we changed onto the San'yō Line for the four-hour journey to Osaka, which I spent kneeling on newspaper spread on the floor.

At the hospital, I was made to walk along a crowded corridor wearing only my shorts, with the other patients all staring at me. I wanted to hide my withered right leg, not show it to everyone! I was silently crying out for my mother to come and rescue me.

When I started elementary school, I had to walk about 250 metres from my house to the school, and I couldn't keep up with my classmates. Sometimes I let my mother give me a piggyback, even though I could walk if I made the effort. But in my heart, I was just wishing that I could walk and jump and play with my own legs.

It was a shock when some of my classmates pointed and laughed at me. I went to bed crying and couldn't sleep for hours. I was so ashamed of my bad leg that I gradually stopped walking, with the result that while I was growing, my leg and hip development was impeded.

Thanks to this, while my siblings were all more than 170 centimetres tall, I was only 160 centimetres.

But I took my revenge on my classmates by soaking their textbooks in water whenever they teased me.

Kenzō Abe, my class teacher in the fifth and sixth years of elementary school, admonished my classmates, saying they should help me, and he himself used to carry my bag for me when we went on excursions. Mr Abe always stood up for me, and he was my one and only support.

Enduring all this during my childhood seems to have led me to develop an inner strength that enabled me to bear adversity in later life. Although encountering repeated setbacks, I never felt that I was suffering. Except for once, when my heart was broken...

Rejection and disappearance

In my youth, I experienced the greatest trial of my life. At 22 years old, rejected by the girl I had been in love with since I was in high school, I fell into the depths of despair.

Convinced that the reason was my disability, I lost the will to live.

Early one morning in March, I got on my scooter, intending to drown myself in the sea, and rode off. At Naruto, I took the ferry to Awaji Island. I rode to the north of the island and then took the ferry across to Akashi on the mainland. Without realising it, my hands were steering me towards my elder brother Yoriaki's house in Tokyo. 'Yes, I'll go and tell my brother about wanting to escape from this world,' I thought, and rode on.

In those days, National Route 1, the main arterial road, was just wide enough for two vehicles to pass each other, and there was little room for two-wheelers. As I rode along at about 20 kph, hundreds, no thousands, of heavy trucks roared as they overtook me only inches away. I rode on, past Kyoto, past Lake Hamana and across the River Tenryū. Freezing cold, I pressed ahead, as though possessed. I took frequent rests at the side of the road, but the night cold was killing me. I would stop my scooter and shake myself, stamp my feet and rub my hands in an attempt to get warm. As I approached Hakone Pass, the uphill slope seemed to climb forever, and my spirits flagged.

I stopped at a noodle stall. The truck driver next to me looked at me and said, 'You don't look too well. How far are you going?' 'Tokyo,' I replied. 'It's too dangerous. I'll take you,' he said, and took my scooter and threw it onto the back of a truck with 'Seino Transportation' written on the side. I climbed into the warm passenger seat and soon dozed off.

Afterwards, my eldest brother Hajime went to the head office of Seino Transportation to try to find and thank the man who he was sure had saved my life. But no one came forward, presumably because the drivers were forbidden to pick up passengers.

Anyway, thanks to the truck driver I made it as far as Tokyo, but I didn't know my brother's address, and I just rode around with no idea where to look for him. For the first time I realised how huge Tokyo was. Then I remembered that he lived somewhere near Tokyo Metropolitan University in Meguro, and as I was looking around the neighbourhood of the university I bumped into Kazuko, my brother's wife, who had gone out looking for me. 'Etchan!' she called me by my nickname, 'What are you doing here, out in the cold?' She took me to their house and presently my brother, who had also been out looking for me, came home. 'Fancy coming all the way here from Shikoku!' he said, looking appalled.

My anguish at being rejected by the girl I had been in love with for five years suddenly exploded.

I cried and wailed for about an hour. It was the first time I had ever let anyone see me shed tears. Back home, in turmoil over my disappearance, the news came by telephone that I was in Tokyo, and my father came straight up. He tried his best to console me, taking me back to Osaka by aeroplane (I'd never been on a plane before) and then taking me to the hot spring resort of Sakakibara in Ise, where he had arranged that we would meet up with my mother. We stayed the night there, and I told them, in tears, that I wanted to go to the spirit world where I wouldn't have this wretched body.

Even now I remember my parents' concern and my mother's haggard face.

Thinking about it makes me realise how fortunate I am to have had my family's loving support, and now to have my own precious family, with my wife, my three daughters and four grandchildren.

The author on his motor scooter

My own mission

At the Sakakibara hot spring, my parents suggested my taking a course of spiritual training at Oomoto. 'You've got nothing to lose,' they said.

My home was a meeting place for Oomoto followers, and it seemed there were always meetings going on, but I never joined in any of them. I was very sceptical about religion, believing it had a negative influence on people's lives, exploiting their faith for monetary gain, restricting their freedom with strict commandments, and even launching religious wars.

But coming at this time, when I had come up against the greatest hurdle of my life so far, even losing hope in living, their suggestion proved to be a turning point in my attitude to religion.

I paid a visit to the Oomoto centre in Kameoka on the railway line west out of Kyoto. From the station I could see the lush, wooded grounds in front of me. Entering, I made my way to the main sanctuary with its sweeping tiled roof. This building stands on the site of the sixteenth-century Kameyama Castle, famous as the stronghold of Akechi Mitsuhide, who rebelled against and defeated the Japanese ruler, Oda Nobunaga.

In this green setting of luxuriant, mature trees, away from the outside world, I spent 43 days training. Getting up each morning at five o'clock, cleaning the toilets, praying, listening to lectures ... going about everything with a feeling of devotion, I no longer found cleaning the toilets unpleasant. During this time, I felt that I was revealing my true self in the presence of a great though invisible power. Suspending my disbelief, I absorbed everything with an attitude of humility.

In the evenings, I read the series of books *Notes on Faith* by Hidemaru Deguchi, the husband of the third spiritual leader. I was struck by the authority of his words, and deeply moved.

'Every human being is born into this world with an important mission that only he or she can carry out.'

Coming to these words, I was moved to tears, and felt myself shaking.

How foolish I was to think of dying. I had been wrong.

'Yes, from now on I'll develop my father's business into one of the best in the world!' I thought.

I felt the courage to live my life to the full rise up inside me. Hidemaru's words 'Positivity is heaven; negativity is hell' became my life's motto.

It was Hidemaru who first brought Esperanto to the attention of Oomoto. While a student at Kyoto University, he saw a newspaper announcement about an Esperanto course at nearby Doshisha University and passed it on to Onisaburo. This led to the founding of the 'Oomoto Esperanto Study Group' (now the 'Society for the Popularisation of Esperanto') in 1923.

A book of excerpts from *Notes on Faith* was published in 1966 under the title *In Search of Meaning* and became a best-seller. I must have read my copy hundreds of times, until it fell apart.

Rejection and treasure

My parents started looking for a partner for me.

They arranged a meeting with a young woman who worked at the Oomoto centre. She was of medium build, and radiated grace and generosity. Nothing came of this meeting, however.

I wasn't disheartened. 'Never mind,' I thought, 'there are plenty more fish in the sea!' About six months later, I began seeing an easy-going local girl who wasn't too tall. This didn't work out either and we gradually drifted apart.

Another meeting was arranged, this time with the daughter of an Oomoto follower from Shizuoka. I travelled on slow bumpy trains via Okayama and Nagoya, crossing the River Tenryū, which I had crossed before on my scooter, and finally getting off at Shizuoka Station and making my way to her house. I remember her being a thin, rather delicate-looking young woman. I wasn't particularly attracted to her, and in any case by the time I got back home a telegram had already arrived turning me down.

What I remember most about the journey was the awe-inspiring sight of Mount Fuji on the way home and thinking what a treasure of the world this mountain was, the pride of Japan.

My grandparents, too, had been worrying about my marriage prospects. They had their eye on a girl called Yoshiko Kamada, who was my grandmother's younger sister's granddaughter. It seems they had been making moves since before my disappearance.

My grandfather Senzō, having met her four times and decided that she was a sound young woman, brought her in to work for my father's firm, and she and I became colleagues at Swany.

Yoshiko was the fifth daughter of Eikichi and Hideno Kamada, farmers in Nyūnoyama in the village of Fukue, a little way from our home. She was a charming girl, about 155 centimetres tall and slender, three years younger than me, and had gone to Fukue Junior High School. Apparently, she knew all about my disappearance.

My grandparents encouraged us to spend time together, inviting us to eat special festival food at their house or on some other pretext.

Yoshiko quickly became skilled at sewing, and presently started accompanying me making the rounds of subcontractors. She was efficient at counting the pieces, loading them on to the truck, and dealing with the subcontractors. Her only fault was that she could sometimes seem slightly aloof.

One day, my grandparents asked me, 'What do you think of Yoshiko?' 'She's a nice girl,' I replied, honestly. 'Well then, you tell her yourself,' my grandfather said.

'Tell her you'll make her happy even though you've got a bad leg. Go on, convince her.'

His urging made me keenly aware how terrified I was of failure. Although I had done spiritual training and thought I had come out of it a new person, I still hadn't got over the trauma of my first heartbreak. That was why all the meetings so far had come to nothing. Even now it moves me to think of how my grandparents recognised my vulnerability and encouraged me.

One evening, I invited Yoshiko to the beach, and lay down beside her. I may not have got full marks, but, helped by the fact that it was dark, and we couldn't see each other's faces, I managed to say what my grandfather had told me.

I held her hand and felt no resistance. I was intoxicated by our first, fumbling kiss.

We have now been together more than fifty years. All I can say to my wife is 'Thank you.'

The author with bride Yoshiko Kamada, 1963

3. Finding new markets

The Kagawa glove industry

Kagawa is one of the four prefectures of the island of Shikoku, but it occupies only one-tenth of its area – less than 2,000 km^2. Into this area is crowded a population of about a million people, many engaged in making the various local products, which include cotton, sugar, salt, rice, gloves, lacquerware, soy sauce and fans. In recent years, new specialities such as 'olive-fed beef' and 'olive-fed yellowtail fish' have become famous.

Glove-making in Kagawa goes back to a certain Futago Shunrei, who was the priest at the Buddhist Senkōji Temple in Fukue Village. He left his temple and returned to lay life around the turn of the twentieth century and learned glove-making in Osaka. His apprentice and successor Tatsukichi Tanatsugu returned to Kagawa in 1900 and founded a company called Sekizen Shōkai. This was the first glove factory in the area.

The local industry expanded when large orders came in from Britain during World War I, and Shirotori developed as a 'glove town'. The industry spread to neighbouring Hiketa and Ōchi, and two companies in particular, Osaka Gloves and Tōyō Gloves, became well established in the area. At the close of the war in 1918, it is recorded that the number of pairs of gloves produced was '730,000 dozen'.

The rise of glove-making to the position of top local industry was supported by the dexterity and skill of women workers in cutting, decoration, sewing, and finishing.

In 1950, Emperor Showa visited Shirotori during a tour of Shikoku, and an annual 'glove festival' was initiated to commemorate the event. Exports began to increase again, and the town regained the prosperity of the pre-war years. Conditions took a turn for the worse following the so-called 'Nixon shock', the anti-inflationary measures announced in 1971 by US President Richard Nixon and the subsequent depreciation of the US dollar to ¥200, which damaged the industry's competitiveness, while a rise in labour costs made things worse.

Glove-making being an unavoidably labour-intensive industry, many companies responded by moving their production overseas and, by 2008, 78 firms affiliated to the Japan Gloves Industrial Association, or about 80%, had moved into countries such as China, Vietnam, and Indonesia. But the number of businesses has now fallen to fewer than 70, while their combined yearly turnover has dropped from ¥66 billion in 1991 to just ¥35 billion at the time of writing.

As well as being labour-intensive, the glove industry is also saddled with the fact that its core product is a seasonal one that people only buy in the winter months, even allowing for the wide range of specialist products such as skiing gloves, sun-protection gloves, marine gloves, baseball gloves, wedding gloves and so on. Some companies have sought new opportunities in such products as leather wallets and luxury bags and established a brand presence in these areas.

How did Swany, my company, respond to this challenge?

Swany is born

After we started exporting, we came up against the problem of our company name. We couldn't get people abroad to pronounce the old name 'Miyoshi Textiles' correctly – it always came out as 'My-yo-shee' (it should be 'Mee-yo-shee'), and we decided that our brand lacked recognisability.

In 1968, we announced a competition within the company, with a prize for the winner, which resulted in 150 ideas for the new name. The winning entry came from a long-time member of the company, Hatsuo Matsumura. His idea for a new name, 'Swany', came from the name of the town Shirotori (which literally means 'white bird' or 'swan'). Looking in the New York telephone directory, he found many Swanees (as in 'Swanee River'), but no Swany. Like 'Sony', 'Sunny' (the Nissan car) and 'Suntory' (the whisky), it was easy to pronounce and had a nice ring to it.

The company had started to penetrate overseas markets in 1959, when it began exporting via an export brokerage company in Kobe. My first trip abroad as a senior executive director came five years later, in 1964. At the same time, the company relocated its premises from our house on the seashore to a site adjoining the Takamatsu-Tokushima railway line and began to expand rapidly.

I shall come back to these developments in detail later on, but here is an outline of the course of Swany's history.

1968-70: Swany Ikeda, Swany Tokushima and Swany Kōchi are established, with a production workforce of 200.

1972-78: Swany Korea, Swany Orient and Swany Asia are established in Korea, with a workforce of 1,200 producing gloves of all kinds.

1980: Swany America is set up in New York, selling to retail outlets.

1984-89: Swany China, Swany Great Wall, Swany Glove and Swany Taicang are established in three cities in the Shanghai region, with a production force of 1,500.

1989: Swany brand skiing gloves go on sale in the USA, reaching annual sales of ¥1 billion. From 2012, sales are the highest in the USA for seven years running.

1997: The body-supporting 'Swany Bag' is launched and becomes a hit product with 110,000 sold every year.

2012: Swany Cambodia is set up in Cambodia with about 300 employees but struggles to remain profitable.

2014: Launch of the world's smallest folding wheelchair, the 'Swany Mini' on the purchasing market, with approximately 1,000 sold every year. In 2020, the Swany Mini makes its appearance on the much larger rental market, 10 times the size of the purchasing market. Japanese, Chinese and US patents obtained.

2018: Swany skiing gloves are launched on the Japanese market. In the dress glove market, the Elmer brand is established.

Revolutionary cost-cutting strategy

The experience of being beaten down on price while out with my father meeting clients made me decide to work on cost reduction. When cutting leather gloves, we used to start by placing a 28-centimetre square glass plate on to a sheet of leather and cutting round it with a knife. Then, we placed a die onto this square, and cut out the glove shape, or 'trank', using a pressure cutter. By directly cutting out the trank with the die, dispensing with the process of first cutting round the glass plate, I could reduce the loss of leather, which accounted for 60% of the cost, by 2%, the difference in size between the die and the plate. This streamlining of the cutting process also increased speed, and the whole industry has now come to adopt the same method.

The key to success lay in the technique of cutting the fourchettes – the narrow strips joining the fronts and backs of the fingers – from the leather left over after cutting out the trank. Twelve fourchettes are needed for one pair of gloves. By being creative, it was possible to get three fourchettes from a piece of waste leather that had previously only yielded two, or to get two from another piece that had only been enough for one. Overall, we managed to obtain an increase of 30-40% of fourchettes. This represented a significant additional profit of about 3% on an average net profit for the industry of 4-5%.

When I first got involved in the glove-making process, we had nine cutting machines, large and small. These were fixed to the concrete floor and connected to the motor by a belt. Because the rotating belt was dangerous, I had the motor fixed on top of the cutting machine and connected directly by means of a V-belt. Isamu Nakagawa, the head of Nakagawa Iron Works, who undertook the conversion for us, liked my idea, because the machines could be operated safely as soon as the power was connected, and all the machines were converted to my method.

We also improved the finishing process. We used to stretch the gloves over a gas-heated glove-shaped copper plate and stretch the leather so that the fingers were neatly straightened. Then, taking two pairs at a time, we would lay the gloves out on cardboard to a few dozen layers' thickness and cover them with a concrete block, and we would leave them like this until the following morning. This was dangerous, however, as it sometimes fell over.

I created a pedal-operated finishing bench with a 70 kg cast metal weight, which was lifted about 3 cm by pressing down on the pedal so that the neatly straightened gloves could be inserted into the space. About the size of a sewing machine table and made of steel, it had four pedal-operated weights. I took satisfaction in this invention, which expressed my aesthetic sense and my love of machinery.

From this time on, my father took responsibility for negotiating with clients, while I was left in charge of cost control. My father must have been pleased with my performance, because he started saying things like 'If it's Etsuo's idea, it must be right.'

Five years after I started working for the company, I was promoted to Senior Executive Director. The more I applied myself to solving problems, the lower our costs became, and the more gloves we sold. I was enjoying my job.

Murky world of export

The winter of 1958, the year I joined the company, was a mild one, and gloves did not sell. We let all our staff go in January, and for three months the whole industry existed on unemployment benefit, until the whole workforce returned in April.

In an attempt to overcome this predicament, my parents started street selling, and for about a month they travelled around Osaka, Kobe, and Okayama, standing on windy street corners calling out 'Gloves! Gloves! Does anyone need any gloves?'

My father went to Kobe every day to try to break into the overseas market, and succeeded in gaining entry to Strong, an export brokerage company, where he was obliged reluctantly to accept the condition of a sweetener of 2% to the section manager in charge. Our first order was for cow skin gloves with rabbit fur lining and with knit lining.

Because Strong were not the makers, they could not reply to the foreign buyers' requests, and so I had to be there at meetings, although I was still an inexperienced youth.

Taking the estimated price in yen of one dozen pairs, I calculated the price with a margin of 30% plus 5% as Strong's commission and divided this by ¥360 to give the shipping price in dollars. I also learned to say 'FOB Kobe' to indicate how far we were responsible for the goods.

One day, a buyer asked me, in English, 'What do you think?' When I hesitated, he pressed me, 'What is your opinion?' I replied boldly, 'Brown is better than black.' 'You're a smart boy,' said the buyer. I felt as if I'd ascended to Heaven. I began to go for lunch with the buyers, and I even went with them to bars and cabarets.

During meetings, I noticed that the buyers were waiting impatiently for me to work out the selling price. After much thought, I devised an index, adding the costs of the face and lining materials, labour, and packaging, with our 30% margin and Strong's 5%. Using an abacus for addition and a slide rule for multiplication, I could convert our cost to the selling price in dollars in an instant.

If our margin added on to production cost was 30%, the index when converted at \$1=¥360 would be 430%; if 31%, 435%; and if 32%, 440%. While observing the buyers' facial expressions, I moved the margin rate up and down and noted their reaction. At just the right time, I would press them, saying 'This is a good time to buy.' In this way, I secured orders for 800 or 1,000 dozen pairs one after another.

Having achieved one result, I would move to the next style. While the jokes were flying around, I would ask how many styles they were planning to buy, trying to get as big a contract as possible.

Milton Schwartz of Avon Glove (right)
with Mr Brown, manager of Strong, 1960

When the buyers came visiting, people from rival companies would be there at Strong's office, bearing samples. Sometimes I had to compete with them, and I would tremble, fearful that the section manager in charge would be bombarded with sweeteners.

On the day of a meeting with Milton Schwartz, CEO of Avon Glove Corporation of New York, four companies did the entertaining. After dinner, we took him to a cabaret, and there was a woman who spoke English well.

Milton was charmed by this woman with her fair complexion and slender face and her fluent English. I was a bit uneasy about her having been brought along for ¥1,000 each from the four companies. I have no memory of how the section manager's sweetener or the unreceipted expenses were accounted for. Many times, I have wanted to ask my father if there wasn't a slightly more reputable way of doing business – but he is no longer around to ask.

Business world tour

In 1964, the year of the Tokyo Olympics, restrictions on overseas travel were lifted, and I went abroad for the first time. The maximum $500 in foreign currency we were allowed to take out of the country would not cover the cost of interpreting, and I made daily trips to the Takamatsu Branch of the Bank of Japan to get $2,000 (¥720,000). With my round-the-world ticket, which cost about ¥700,000, I took off from Haneda Airport in Tokyo, a bundle of nerves.

On top of the Empire State
Building, 1964

The next morning, after arriving in New York, I went to a café next to the Prince George Hotel where I was staying, and asked for 'hot milk, toast, and lemon tea'. The server didn't seem to understand a word of this, so I repeated it over and over again, getting redder in the face each time. While this was going on, a Japanese student came in, and, seeing that I was having trouble, corrected my Japanese English for me: '*hat* milk, *tea with lemon*'. By this time, I was dripping with sweat.

I went to the towering Chamber of Commerce building with my interpreter, who I had hired through the travel agent for $25 a day (about ¥9,000). There, a huge middle-aged man with a ruddy complexion searched for glove companies for me, and gave me a list of about 30 companies, with telephone numbers. I was impressed with how courteously he helped me, a complete stranger from Japan.

First, I called the NY Merchandise Company from a public telephone. At first, they said that they weren't interested in importing because they only sold in small quantities, but my interpreter persisted, 'We'll only take five minutes of your time.' We met the boss, a short mild-mannered man who seemed very pleasant, but he just glanced at my samples and showed no interest, and we were out of there in just ten minutes.

I was turned down again at the next company we visited, and we then turned to the third company on our list, Gelmart, a company selling knitted gloves. Here, too, I was told 'We're not interested in leather gloves.' But when I showed them my samples, they said, 'Why don't you take these to IBC?' and kindly wrote down the company's address and the CEO's name. Unfortunately, the CEO was away on business, so I just made a note of the company for a future visit.

I struggled to get an appointment at the fourth company, only to find that they only sold work gloves. In nine days, I approached 30 companies, and got to meet with fewer than a third of them. Many were businesses dealing in work gloves or knitted gloves. These were the only ones they found for me in the Companies Yearbook, so there was nothing I could do. Of those I did meet, only NY Merchandise eventually opened an account with us some years later.

Disappointed at the miserable result of my efforts in New York, I left for Germany, on a Pan Am flight bound for Hamburg. There were no other Japanese passengers on board. I made my way to the toilet, and, not knowing that the lock was broken, touched the door causing it to swing open. An angry woman's voice yelled from inside 'How dare you!' to my great embarrassment.

At the Hotel Atlantic on the banks of Lake Alster, unable to read the German or English names of the dishes on the menu, I pointed to the first item, and was brought some vegetable soup. I then tried the second item, and this time I was brought a consommé. Thinking it was time for the main course, I tried pointing at the bottom item, and was informed 'That's the name of the restaurant.'

That night, I got into bed, but I immediately started worrying about whether I could find an interpreter the next day, and I ended up even worrying if I would ever be able to return home to Japan. I couldn't sleep at all because of my jet lag. By the time morning came, I was in tears.

While in Hamburg, I visited the Chamber of Commerce with my interpreter, who, I was told, was 'a former trading company employee'. Armed with a list of about ten companies who looked likely to be in the glove business, I spent the next two days visiting them, but not one was interested in importing gloves.

Near the hotel, I discovered a sign with the name 'Kogetsu' in Japanese characters. It turned out to be a Japanese restaurant, very rare in those days. With great excitement, I went in, and ate a meal of sashimi. On the shelf was a row of Japanese books like the samurai novel *Musashi* by Eiji Yoshikawa, and the other customers were reading them absorbedly.

At my next destination, London, I ran around in the same way, but failed to find any potential customers. In deep despondency, I flew on to my final destination, Milan in Italy. In my bathroom at the Meridian Hotel where I stayed, I sat astride the washbasin next to the toilet and turned the tap. A jet of boiling hot water shot up, giving me a nasty scald. I should have used the cold tap to adjust the temperature of the water. I was stinging for a few days afterwards, but fortunately I managed to get back to Japan in one piece.

In the lonely month I spent travelling, I had struggled with the language barrier, different food, jet lag and culture shock. Arriving back at Haneda, I felt as if my feet weren't touching the ground, as if I were sleepwalking.

Struggling with English

The experience of my foreign travels convinced me that I would get nowhere without a command of English.

First, I followed the NHK radio programme *English Conversation*, with instructors Katsuaki Tōgo and Helen Reynolds. The textbook cost only ¥120 a month. I went over the lessons with enthusiasm, repeating everything twice over. When I was away on business, my wife recorded the programmes for me.

In the car, as soon as I started the engine, I listened to President Kennedy's speeches on a tape loop. Over about three years I must have played it thousands of times, speaking out loud along with the tape. It was way too advanced for me, but it proved to be useful in future meetings.

While I was away on business, I listened on stereo earphones, and mumbled away, not caring where I was, practising my pronunciation.

Once, I was on a Hankyu Line train from Takarazuka to Umeda Station in Osaka. After a while, I removed the earphones and heard the announcement 'Takarazuka! Takarazuka!' I looked round, and the lady sitting next to me told me that I hadn't got off the train at Umeda. I was so engrossed in my English study that I'd come all the way back to where I'd started without noticing. Much to my embarrassment, a student who was on the train started to laugh out loud. I wanted the ground to swallow me up.

Something similar happened when I was on a plane going to Boston. While I sat there, immersed in my English, a flight attendant came and started yelling at me excitedly. Hurry up and get off the plane, she was saying. Wondering what the matter was, I looked round to find that we had already landed, and all the other passengers had gone. After struggling like this for four years, I felt I could conduct business – only just, though...

In 1968, four years after my first visit to the United States, I entered the Kobe branch of Berlitz, the world's leading language school, for a one-month crash course to finish off my studies. The tuition fees were about ¥1,000,000. The Kobe school was a newly opened campus, and I had four foreign instructors. I spent ten hours a day studying, with 40-minute lessons followed by a five-minute break. At night I dreamed in English. I went for lunch with my teachers. I especially enjoyed having lunch with Judy Smith, a charming teacher from Australia.

My determination and tenacity, as well as patience and effort, were what kept me going in my drive to master this language. For four years, I devoted myself body and soul to learning English. I believe it was a worthwhile investment. If I couldn't speak English, I believed it would be a huge brake on Swany's efforts at overseas expansion.

I put a lot of effort into my speaking ability, but one day, when I was approaching the age of 80, the telephone rang.

'Are you Mr Miyoshi?'

'Yes, yes, momenton, ĉu vi estas... (wait a moment, is that...)' I found myself replying in Esperanto, which I had recently been studying. The English words wouldn't come. Such was the state of my English after not keeping it up for ten years.

I'm not making myself understood

I had studied English zealously, but I still found it hard to get out of my Japanese pronunciation habits.

On my third trip to America, I was in Chicago, and I went for something to eat. I asked the server for spaghetti, but she just looked at me with a perplexed expression. I tried over and over again, but I couldn't get my meaning across. She brought the cook to my table, and when I tried again, the cook nodded, 'Oh, spa*ghe*tti!' and I was able to get my lunch. It seemed the problem was my failure to put a strong accent on the 'ghe'.

On a plane from New York, a lady once asked me 'Where are you going?' 'I'm going to Canada,' I replied. 'Where?' 'Canada.' 'What did you say?' 'I said, "Canada."' 'Where's Canada?' 'Canada, Ca-na-da, you know?' 'I don't know. You don't mean *Canada*, do you?'

Once, I was on my way to The Cathedral of St. John the Divine, the largest church in New York. I hailed a taxi and asked the driver for 'Amsterdam Avenue'. The driver looked puzzled. I tried again and again but to no avail. Get in front, the driver finally said, opening the door for me. In New York taxis, the driver's seat was separated from the back of the taxi by a partition of iron bars to protect the driver. I got in the front seat and showed the driver my map. 'Oh, *Am*-ster-*dam*,' he said. I realised that I should have been putting a strong accent on the 'Am' and the 'dam'.

Where I was confident was in numbers and in glove-related vocabulary. In Japanese, instead of 'million' (a thousand thousand) and 'billion' (a thousand million), we express large numbers in units of *man* (ten thousand), *oku* (ten thousand times ten thousand = 100,000,000) and so on. To make it easier to use large numbers in English, I drummed it into my head that the population of Japan (one *oku*) was 'one hundred million', and the population of China (ten *oku*) was 'one billion'. By thinking of large numbers as multiples of the population of Japan or China, I was able easily to understand and use the English numbers.

But the one word that gave me the most trouble of all was 'glove'.

How on earth could I pronounce that word so that people would understand me?

Cutting out the broker – a dream come true

On my third visit to America, I finally realised my dream of trading directly without going through an agent.

This came about through a telephone call to Milton Schwartz, CEO of Avon Glove Corporation, who I had met when he was in Japan. 'Hey, is that Etsuo? I'm only a few minutes away from your hotel. Come over right away,' he said. This was when we were still doing business with Strong, the export brokers in Kobe, before Swany started trading directly.

When we met, I said to him, 'I couldn't send a telex because I didn't want Strong to know.' 'Why not?' he said. 'Do you mean that section manager? He got fired for taking sweeteners. In a way, it's thanks to that company that we've been trading all this time. But their staff management is dreadful. I must have lost a fortune thanks to that rascal. How much were you paying him?'

I didn't know what to say. He continued, 'I was paying them 5% commission, and on top of that it turns out he was taking sweeteners from you. What an utter scoundrel.' Again, I was at a loss what to say. 'Since you've come to see me, I suppose you're still keen on doing business. If we link up, it'll make us more competitive. Don't you agree?'

I replied, 'Oh, we only gave him pocket money.' I didn't say it was a whole 2%. If I'd told him the truth and he'd found out just how much he might have saved on the price of our gloves if we hadn't been making these payments, he would have had a fit.

I stayed silent, looking into his eyes. After a while, Milton relaxed and said, 'Never mind that! Let's start business.' He must have been impressed by the quality of Swany's products. I gave him some quotes, and he gave me some orders.

This was the moment when we began trading directly, without going through an agent.

I don't remember how much the orders were for now. Milton said, 'Your English is not perfect, but if we can see the actual goods, we'll do fine.' Nodding to the interpreter, he said, 'We won't be needing an interpreter from now on.'

I exchanged handshakes with Milton's brother Bob and all the office staff. There were just six people in the office, but I was told that a few dozen more were employed at the distribution depot. I learned that this was the typical pattern for a New York importer, with headquarters in Manhattan controlling shipments from a warehouse in the suburbs.

'Next time I'll invite you to my house. Keep up the English,' he said with a firm handshake before we parted. I felt tears of joy coming to my eyes.

Nightlife

When writing this book, I put in a telephone call to Tokuichi Shikatani, the President of our competitor Fuji Industries, hoping to find out more about the circumstances of the dismissal of the section manager at Strong, half a century ago. He told me that the section manager had demanded 5%, but they had beaten him down to 2%. It seemed that he had been pocketing 2% each from four companies. With all that money he could have bought a few dozen apartments.

Apparently, Strong's Director approached Mr Shikatani, and asked him, 'I hear from Miyoshi Textiles that Section Manager M has been taking sweeteners. Have you been paying him, too?' When Mr Shikatani replied that he had, the Director made the on-the-spot decision to fire the section manager, saying, 'I see. We'll dismiss him this afternoon.' I had a gut feeling that my father had appealed to Strong's Director out of concern about involving me in these 'murky' activities.

There were three men and one woman working under the glove section manager at Strong. The section manager and the woman always used to go straight home after work, and I used to have dinner with the other three men, after which we would visit bars and cabarets.

We used to frequent a cabaret in the Sannomiya district of Kobe called the New Century. One night, when the drink was starting to flow, the curtain that covered the ceiling caught fire. A panic broke out, and a voice repeatedly announced, 'Will staff please escort the customers to safety.' I followed our hostesses, but they led us into the changing room, which was full of people chaotically searching for their belongings. No one was guiding us out of the building, so I quickly attached myself to another group and we were able to get out.

When they came to my native Kagawa, I showed them the neon lights of Takamatsu, and took them to a large establishment called the Rainbow Garden Cabaret.

The famous singer Izumi Yukimura was there, and she sang her hit songs *East of Eden* and *Love Is a Many-splendored Thing*. Frank Nagai, another popular singer, also appeared, singing his hit song *Kimi koishi* ('I yearn for you') in his sweet baritone voice.

Developing new markets with broken English

I toured the world every year to expand our markets, hiring interpreters wherever I went. Because of the disability in my right leg, carrying my luggage in a suitcase with no wheels was agony. Moving forward step by step, like a tortoise, I went from meeting to meeting, my head crammed full of English glove jargon.

True to his word, CEO Schwartz invited me to his house. After drinks, we went over to the dinner table. Ms Schwartz, carrying a casserole, said something to me that sounded like 'Upside down, please!' I couldn't understand what she meant and didn't know what to do. Milton came to the rescue and explained with gestures that she wanted me to turn my plate over.

After he had had a few drinks, Milton asked me, 'Are you selling to big glove companies like Grandoe and Fownes? They're based in a little place called Gloversville about a hundred miles north of New York City. They're not competing with me, so why not go along there?'

Gloversville NY began as a settlement of immigrant glove-makers from Europe in the 16th and 17th centuries. Before the war there were 300 glove companies in the town, but now there were only about ten. The town's population had also decreased by about a third to 15,000, comparable with my hometown of Higashikagawa. There is also a Tannersville and a Huntersville.

When I first visited Grandoe Corporation, they told me that they were manufacturing all the gloves they needed at their factories in Puerto Rico and the Philippines, and they had no plans to buy from other companies.

However, when I visited them the fourth time, CEO Richard Zuckerwar treated me to a deluxe hamburger, and told me that he liked our soft synthetic leather Jelmin, but that our knit-lined, pile-lined and rabbit fur-lined gloves were too expensive. It was a critical moment.

This was the year in which Swany Korea was getting under way, enabling us to reduce prices by about 10%, and we succeeded in securing an order for 35,000 dozen pairs at an average price of $25 a dozen. At the time one dollar was worth ¥250, and this was Swany's first large contract worth more than ¥200,000,000.

Richard and his wife Susan came to Japan on their honeymoon, and we took them sightseeing to the famous Ritsurin Gardens and Yashima with its panoramic view of the Seto Inland Sea. We became family friends, but two years later Richard and Susan divorced.

Westerner size

For ten years, I kept up our approaches to the major glove manufacturer Fownes Brothers, and although we didn't achieve the breakthrough we hoped for, I was given the opportunity to see their factory in the Philippines. When I visited, there was one open factory space with 2,000 people making leather gloves. The production area and the office were separated by an all-glass partition, and the whole area and all the employees could also be seen from the director's room on the upstairs floor. In the corner, there was a shower with cold water only, because, I was told, it was summer all year round and they didn't need hot water.

The director talked about how easy managing the factory was, but, perhaps because they saw me as a competitor, they wouldn't let me inspect the production area. The average monthly wage there was $20 (¥7,200), lower than at Swany Korea, where it was ¥8,100. I understood why the retail price had not gone up for many years.

Having heard from him that the Gold Glove Company, a Canadian company, were making gloves in Manila, I flew to Montreal, where they were based. Third-generation CEO Danny Gold, finding that we were the same age, and hearing about my relationship with Grandoe, showed a lot of interest. He told me, however, that on Swany's gloves the thumb was too close to the base of the four fingers, which made opening one's hands uncomfortable. He also wanted the junior and children's sizes fixed, and resolving these two issues was their condition for doing business.

He told me to make men's size L 3% larger than size M, and size XL 6% larger. Size S should be 3% smaller. Junior size L should be 93% the size of men's size M, junior size M should be 90%, and junior size S should be 87%. As for children's sizes, L, M and S should be 83%, 80% and 77% respectively, while infant sizes should be 73%, 70% and 67%. The cuffs for the junior sizes should be made 3% wider, for the children's sizes 6% wider, and for the infant sizes 9% wider. For the Japanese market, taking these one size down worked perfectly.

Danny also gave me paper patterns, which allowed for the stretch of the leather. After we followed his advice, our sales grew appreciably.

European importers

Kauko, an import agent in Helsinki, the Finnish capital, were acting as intermediaries for department stores. After convincing my contact, Mr Kajoste, that I, a person with a disability, could be a senior executive director, and that we were a decent sized company capable of supplying gloves in sizes matching European hands, I passed the test.

In Finland, there has long been a direct selling system in place for supplying the main department stores such as Stockmann, Sokos and Kesko. We received sample orders and were able to secure contracts mainly for lined ox leather and lined split leather gloves. By means of a 'letter of credit' issued by the customer's bank, we could receive payment immediately after shipment, and Kauko were guaranteed 5% of the transaction value.

It was so cold out in the car park that the car door would freeze while we were meeting, so I had to leave the engine running. In winter, the temperature fell below -30°C. It didn't start to get light until 9am and it got dark again at 3pm. Cars kept their lights on all day, and the children shone torches on the path on their way to kindergarten.

In Finland, which had a history of oppression under the Russian Empire, Japan was admired for having won the Russo-Japanese War of 1904-1905, and the Japanese Admiral Tōgō was celebrated as a hero. My success there might have been helped by this pro-Japanese sympathy as well as my arriving in Northern Europe ahead of our competitors.

I visited Aug. Eklöw in Stockholm, the Swedish capital, every time I went to Europe.

Later, I had an appointment for a business meeting with the President of Eklöw at the Royal Hotel in Osaka, but I misheard and was waiting for him at the Royal Hotel in Kobe. The President was furious and told me over the phone that he wanted no more to do with us.

Some years later, I had left a meeting with another Swedish company, and was down in the lobby of the building. The Stockholm taxi drivers had gone on strike, and while I was wondering how I would get to my next meeting, I saw a post van pull up outside. 'Please help me! Please take me to the Swedish Co-operative Association!' I begged. 'You must be joking, this is a post van, not a taxi,' the driver said, waving me away. The driver had a valid point. The van was indeed not a taxi. But I implored him, putting my hands together in an attitude of prayer. Perhaps noticing my disability and sympathising with me, he relented and let me get in.

'Don't tell anyone about this!' he commanded me. This lucky lift in the post van led to our opening an account with the Swedish Co-op, who were customers of Eklöw.

The President of the Italian company AGAM was Mr Chiodi. He came to Japan every spring and autumn. He encouraged me when I was following a fasting regime for a kidney problem, and he himself observed a brown rice diet, keeping up a hardworking schedule on just one evening meal a day. His secret, he said, was to swim 500 metres a day. He urged me to swim to keep fit, and, following his advice, I made it my daily routine to swim 250 metres.

My experiences during this time were most valuable, allowing me to become acquainted with the European business environment while learning about new countries and their cultures.

Sears, the world's top department store

Around 1975, the leading European and American department store chains began directly importing from Asian countries. I made a survey of department stores, their sales rankings, and their characteristic features, and compiled a list, asking the receptionists for the names of their buyers.

I made a telephone call to Mr Graf of the Boston department store Zayre, ranked 17th. 'We're doing fine already,' Mr Graf told me, and promptly ended the call. I tried calling again, but he just said, 'Stop calling!' I made one desperate last attempt, calling from reception and asking for just five minutes of his time. 'No! How many times do I have to tell you?' he shouted back. But I persisted, 'I might have some information about Japan that would be useful to you.'

'Just five minutes, and I mean it!' he said, and I went up to his room. When I saw him, I confess I was surprised to see an African American, nothing like the image I had formed of him in my mind, and I hesitated in front of him. I was inexperienced. I should have known never to act surprised when meeting someone for the first time!

An hour passed by. To my joy, he told me that he liked our products and our prices. Later, he visited us in Shikoku, and we started doing business together. In my experience, when turning up without an appointment I managed to get an interview about half of the time, and when I did, I often got a good result.

Number 15 on my list was Korvettes in New York. We finally started doing business with them after my 13th effort. We managed to open an account with them when the third buyer, another African American, had taken over. A tall man with a strong nose, he had the (for me) hard-to-pronounce name Fitzpatrick, and my poor pronunciation led more than once to the telephone operator giving up on me and cutting me off.

After a while, I learned to pronounce the syllable 'pa' of Fitzpatrick with extra stress. As for the spelling, I managed to learn it after practising writing the name out about five times.

My efforts at selling to Sears, the biggest department store in the world with a yearly turnover of five trillion yen and a workforce of 400,000, took seven years and more than 20 visits to Chicago. Four times a year I kept going back, and things reached the point where I was troubled by dreams of the roar of the jet engine, and Yoshiko started to worry about me. Sears' headquarters was a group of buildings scattered over a wide area. Overwhelmed by the authority of the world number one store, I felt myself going weak at the knees.

I laid out my samples on a desk in the buyer's room, a small room only about ten feet square. Mr Hanson, a man of average size, picked up a glove and asked, 'How much?' '$25.40.' 'What's the face material?' 'Jelmin. Made in Japan.' 'Nice and soft. And the lining?' 'Acrylic.' I had been there for about 15 minutes when he gave the sign to leave. 'So sorry! The next supplier is waiting!' I met this man four or five times, but he never gave me a chance.

I still visited Sears four times a year. Two years later, Mr Hanson had been replaced by a towering man with narrow, blue eyes, called Mr Stewart. I didn't know what had happened to Mr Hanson, but in any case, I wasn't given a chance.

In the sixth year, I met a third buyer, Mr Bridges. It turned out that we were both amateur radio operators, and we had a lively chat about our shared hobby. A smallish man, he had a habit of mumbling when he talked, but he was a good listener. He had a serious, sincere attitude. He seemed impressed with my perseverance in visiting them for six years, and he later came to see us in Shikoku and also at our factory in Korea. Meeting in Seoul, in the seventh year since I first approached Sears, we struck a deal worth more than ¥200 million a year.

When we established Swany America in 1980, this Tom Bridges became Vice President, and he played a vital role there. His contribution to breaking down the cultural barriers was immeasurable.

Tom retired in 2004, but we have kept up our friendship with Tom and his lovely wife Judy and her father, and we were invited to their daughter's wedding.

An invitation from the CEO of Sears

In 1982, the CEO of Sears and his wife came to Japan, and about 500 suppliers were invited to a reception at the grand Hotel Okura. It was a glittering gathering of the rich and famous, including Seiji Tsutsumi, Chairman of the Seibu Group.

The good-natured-looking Mr and Ms Swift stood at the entrance and greeted all the attendees with handshakes. By the time I entered, half an hour had already passed. 'And what are you supplying us with?' Mr Swift asked. 'Gloves,' I replied. 'Pardon, what was that?' 'Gloves.' 'I'm sorry, I don't understand.' 'Winter gloves,' I said, miming with my hands.

'Ah, gloves!' he said, beaming. I had trouble getting through to him with my English, but I was delighted that an insignificant supplier like me was there as an invited guest. I remembered my many trips to Chicago in sun, rain, wind and snow and the roar of the jet engines.

'I've done it!' I cried out in my heart. I could feel the tears starting to well up. If there hadn't been anyone else there, I would have cried out loud, but I controlled myself, and after shaking hands with Ms Swift, I moved on.

4. The holy grail – a year-round producte

Rocky path

With its global expansion, Swany's sales grew steadily. But freeing itself from the glove industry's fatal flaw, its reliance on a seasonal product that sells only in winter, was not easy.

Frequently, work would stop at our factories because there weren't enough orders to keep us busy during the quiet period from December to March. Starting in the 1970s, I spent the month of July based in New York and visiting five or six other cities, hoping to get orders. This would give time for procurement of materials and inspection of samples before the start of the slack season.

I travelled every day to the head office of Fownes in New York, whose factory in Manila I had seen. Their Vice President, Mr Gluckman, saw me as a competitor, but I hoped that he would be brought round by our quality and our prices. However, after seven or eight years without making any progress, I could see that I was just handing them useful information about the industry, and I decided that I had to give up.

Aris Gloves of Fifth Avenue spent hundreds of millions of yen every year on TV advertising and had been highly successful with their Isotoner 'one size fits all' stretch gloves that don't slip on the steering wheel. The Isotoner brand became a world leader, with the claim that they 'liberated Americans from the cold steering wheel'.

I regularly visited my contact Mr Harman here at seven o'clock when he arrived at work, but for some reason we were not making progress. I kept going for six or seven years, deciding that the early mornings could be put to good use... He later applied for the job of Vice President of Swany America, but the conditions were not right and instead we appointed Tom Bridges, who I mentioned in the last chapter.

The American manufacturer Gates was controlled by a good-natured gentleman, Mr Nessel. I travelled by train to see him at their head office in Gloversville. Mr Nessel often brought the conversation round to family and golf, and I wondered why he was so keen on talking about these subjects, but I realised he was just being normally friendly. He was placing orders with glove makers in East Asia for 3,000 dozen pairs a year (worth about ¥150 million) of skiing gloves made of lightweight polypropylene material with thick lining.

Mr Nessel held out for a 10% price reduction on our $25 gloves and wanted a decision by the end of July. This was a massive reduction. Two weeks after I returned to Japan, he asked me to come to Seattle.

Outbound, economy class was fully booked, so for the first time in my life I flew first class, and he met me at the airport. Half of his order was to be for March shipment, but the other half was to be for September shipment, which would mean warehouse charges. But at least our factories would still be operating.

Our business model was to aim for an average net profit of 5-6%, by recouping the losses of the slack period in the busy period.

My strategy came to be accepted with time, but my call for a price increase of 10% on additional orders in the busy period was refused. I resisted any price reduction since this would put me at a disadvantage in securing orders for the next quiet season, but in the end, it was only with much difficulty that I was able to manage a profit of 4-5%.

I continued visiting importers New York Glove, Avon Glove, Grandoe, and Monark in Montreal every year. But the number of customers who were prepared to take a risk and buy to stock was limited, and in ten years of trying, I could barely manage to secure two months' worth of orders, or half my goal.

In the southern hemisphere

It was inevitable that Swany would look for work in the quiet season in the southern hemisphere, where the seasons are opposite to those of the northern hemisphere.

With the Managing Director of Dents Gloves and his wife,
1977

In 1977, I met the CEO of Dents Gloves in Sydney, Australia.

I had sent them our company brochure in advance, and this seemed to have had some impact, as on arrival I was surprised to be invited to dine with CEO Gasson and his wife at a Japanese restaurant. The following day's meeting, however, was a big disappointment. They only wanted to order a few dozen pairs of each of our products.

I also visited several companies in Melbourne, and met with a positive initial response, but the outcome was much the same everywhere.

The reasons for this were, first, the fact that it only really gets cold enough to wear gloves in Tasmania and other southern parts of the country, and second, the small population. I suspected that the situation would be the same in South Africa, but I decided not to give up until I had been there and found out for myself.

We touched down in Perth in South-East Australia to refuel en route, crossed the Indian Ocean and flew over Madagascar, an island 1.6 times the size of Japan. Arriving in South Africa, I visited Johannesburg and Cape Town and met representatives of glove businesses in both cities, but I came away with orders for only a few dozen pairs of each product.

Since I had made the journey here, I decided to go and see the Cape of Good Hope. The view from the cliff-top was magnificent and there were no other people around. While I was standing there, feeling alone in this desolate place, a German couple appeared, and the husband took a photo of me with his wife to mark this once-in-a-lifetime encounter.

I left Cape Town and flew to London via Kinshasa in the former Zaire (now DR Congo), but we had to land in Madrid late at night because of thick fog at Heathrow Airport.

At the hotel provided by the travel agent, the porter took my case and left me in my room. As he slammed the door shut, the doorknob fell off and rolled on the floor. I was trapped in my room, unable to open the door. I called the lobby from my phone, but I couldn't make myself understood with my English. In desperation, I cried out 'SOS!', and then someone came and fixed the door for me.

Sadly, despite all my efforts, my tour of the Southern Hemisphere did not result in orders that would keep us busy through the quiet season.

One step forward, one step back

In America, annual sales of Swany brand skiing gloves reached ¥1 billion, and make-to-stock became viable, at least to some extent. This has given us about one month's work in the quiet season, but because these are made in our Chinese factory, we are in a difficult situation at the time of writing, owing to President Trump's retaliatory tariffs.

In 2018, we dispatched Ichiro Kuwahara to Swany America as President. Straight away he aimed at breaking away from seasonal products, turning his attention to cycling gloves.

The greatest market for skiing gloves is around the Rocky Mountains, and in summer there is a market for mountain biking equipment, but because the snow of 2018 did not thaw, the summer 2019 bicycle race could not be held, putting our plans for cycling gloves on hold.

For a half century, our efforts to secure work for the winter season have followed a pattern of one step forward, one step back. Currently, Swany is working on developing gloves for spring and summer sports as one of its most important ventures.

UV gloves for year-round production

Swany were pioneers in the field of UV gloves in Japan, entering this market nearly 40 years ago in 1982. An acquaintance told me that she would like gloves that protected her hands and arms against sunburn. When I mentioned this to my wife Yoshiko, she told me that her friend who works as an insurance representative was saying the same thing to her.

We prepared samples made of thin, UV-protective material in short, medium, and long sizes, and took them to the insurance company's office. The women showed much interest, as we explained that dark colours were better at blocking ultraviolet rays than pale colours. All six of them declared that these gloves were exactly what they wanted.

We hired the Takamatsu Branch of the advertising agency Dentsu to help with the marketing, and we took meticulous care with the packaging.

We gave the product the name 'My Care Lady', punning on the title of the popular musical film *My Fair Lady* starring Audrey Hepburn.

In 1984, Yasushi Okudai, Hidenobu Mitani, Kazumasa Isshiki and Taku Muromaki joined the company.

These four launched a nationwide 'My Care Lady' sales campaign, but disappointingly, many customers pointed out that they were too small, and we had a tough time for four or five years getting rid of our stock.

Yasushi Okudai, who later became President of Swany Cambodia, wrote about this time in *Swany News* in 1999:

When I was sent to Osaka, I went out every day trying to sell 'My Care Lady' gloves. Carrying my samples, I plodded on in the ferocious summer heat, dripping with sweat, trying to interest the ladies at cosmetic companies. I felt like one of the itinerant medicine peddlers of days gone by. I had gone beyond feeling ashamed – I was desperate. But, perhaps out of pity for me, many shops did take the gloves.

Although there is nothing unusual about them now, in those days people simply hadn't heard of sun protection gloves. Foresight is important, but being too far ahead of one's time doesn't help. We were about ten years early with the launch. In the end, despite our best efforts, we withdrew the product, incurring a loss of some tens of millions of yen.

Fifteen years after this, in about 2000, a number of companies launched 'UV gloves', and the product began to gain popularity. Swany, too, is among them, and we now make a million pairs a year. A market worth about 20% of industry sales has taken shape, and these gloves have grown to become a major product, with fierce competition on price. And yet the imbalance towards winter items has not gone away.

'Beyond gloves'

The search continued. In the 1980s, our 'Big Swany' child-to-adult free-size gloves lost out to the competition, and our 'Hot Swany' lined gloves also had to be withdrawn because of flagging sales.

'Yes Swany', our lined knitted gloves in 32 colours packaged in a transparent case, grew to become a major item, selling for more than 10 years, but this was not a year-round product.

In 1985, my youngest brother developed the 'Grip Swany' brand of outdoor leather gloves, which achieved high name recognition among enthusiasts, as I mentioned above.

I began to think that perhaps we hadn't been looking in the right place. We had been sticking to gloves, thinking of Swany as a glove maker and nothing else, whereas in fact we had started out by taking US military surplus tents and using the material to make trousers. There was no reason to cling to gloves to the exclusion of all else – we needed to be more flexible in our thinking.

A hint came from close at hand.

Having a disability in my leg, I found it exhausting heaving a heavy suitcase around on my overseas trips. I embarked on a revolution in luggage, thinking at first only of my personal use. Out of this came the body-supporting 'Swany Bag'. I had found an escape from dependence on a seasonal product.

Later, I developed post-polio syndrome (about which more below), and I was forced to spend three years using a wheelchair. I found conventional wheelchairs hard to manoeuvre, colliding with doors and toilets, and so I decided to design my own compact model, with drive wheels of 40 cm diameter and low enough that the user can grab things on the floor.

I made the drawings and built prototypes, and after investing about ¥10 million, the 'Etsuo Swany' was born.

I entered it in the International Home Care and Rehabilitation Exhibition at the Tokyo Big Sight Exhibition Centre, but although it did attract some attention, not one of the 70 prototypes was sold, and we scrapped all of them except one, which we kept for the company museum. My whole body was shaking, I was so upset. I didn't realise at the time that this failure would ultimately lead to success.

I was keenly aware that our survival depended on our developing products that people really want.

In Part 2 I shall tell the story of the development of our body-supporting luggage and our compact folding wheelchairs, which were to become our flagship products alongside our gloves.

5. Overseas expansion

Growing production at home

How did a small glove maker from Kagawa come to expand onto the world stage?

Swany moved its production overseas because of rising labour costs, a problem any manufacturing business is liable to face. We went abroad looking for skilled staff who would work for us at an affordable cost. There is nothing out of the ordinary about this nowadays, but here again it seems we were ahead of our time, and as a result we came up against resistance and prejudice from nationalists and the media.

When I joined the company in 1960, we were starting to outgrow our factory, and we built a new factory with an area of about 330 m^2 to my father's design, next to our house. The ground floor was the cutting area, and the upstairs floor was the sewing workshop, and the number of staff grew to about 100.

Then the company relocated its premises away from our house on the seashore to a new site, as I mentioned briefly above. In 1964, we bought about 7,500 m^2 of farmland by the side of the Takamatsu-Tokushima railway line for about ¥7,000,000. I designed a factory of about 1,400 m^2, which cost about ¥20 million. All on one floor, it had a central office connected to the production and warehouse areas. It was built by Daiwa House using a steel tube structure to keep costs down.

In 1968, Swany Ikeda was established in the town of Ikeda in neighbouring Tokushima Prefecture, famous for the high school baseball team. The following year we founded Swany Tokushima, on another site in the same town, and the year after that we founded Swany Kōchi below the Sameura Dam in Kōchi Prefecture. As there were not enough workers in the production area around Shirotori, we turned to the central part of Shikoku looking for women from farming villages. Our plan had the intended result, and 200 people came to work at our factories.

The technical side of operations, the cutting and sewing, was under the charge of Yasuo Okada, who had been with us from the beginning, and who would go on to take charge of technology at our factories in Korea and China, while my younger brother Asao took overall control of management.

A difficult problem was keeping control of the supply of leather. It was a condition of survival that we needed to keep the amount of leather used for each pair as low as possible, hiding any scratches to avoid wasting too much. The cutting people tended naturally to take the leather with the fewest scratches, and so before long large quantities of leftover scratched leather were piling up in the warehouse. The supervisor had the critical task of convincing the cutters of the need to save.

Then there was the problem of fixing the rates of performance incentives for each process, such as sewing the thumbs, sewing the fourchettes, sewing together the backs and palms and so on. The sewing workforce were quick to notice the slightest unfairness, and trouble always seemed to start from incentives. Fixing performance incentives continues to be a difficult challenge to this day.

We manufactured leather gloves at our headquarters or at our three factories in Tokushima and Kōchi, while for our fabric and artificial leather products we outsourced the sewing and finishing to subcontractors in Kagawa or Tokushima. These employed a few to a dozen or so people, and reliability regarding quality and delivery was in the hands of the subcontractor. Productivity and quality were also highly sensitive to the design of the glove cutting dies. The patterns I had received from Danny Gold in Canada were put to full use.

Production base moves to Korea

During this phase of expansion, we were starting to lose about 20 to 30% every year to our competitors in Taiwan, and Korea emerged as a candidate for a new production base. My father was of the opinion that since the Korean winter was cold enough to wear gloves, unlike Taiwan, they would produce better gloves there. And so, we decided to throw in our lot with Korea.

The establishment in 1972 of our first overseas factory, Swany Korea, in which we invested $750,000 (about ¥250 million) helped to shield us from the effects of a sudden rise in the value of the yen. Because of the 'Nixon shock' of 1971, which resulted in a rise in the value of the yen against the dollar from ¥360 to ¥240, hundreds of millions of our home company's profits went up in smoke. The damage was however limited to Japan-made materials, and when in 1985 the 'Plaza Accord' of finance ministers and central bank governors led to the US dollar falling by more than ¥80, we were able somehow to withstand the effects. We responded by making efforts to balance imports and exports by increasing imports to Japan.

When starting our venture in Masan in Korea, I decided that the motto 'For self, for society, for the world' should be the company's mission statement. Our ideal should be that while we work for our own benefit, we contribute also to wider society. If we made a pair of gloves at a cost of ¥700 to sell for ¥1,000, we bought them at ¥850 from Swany Korea, thus sharing the profit between Korea and Japan. With this policy of profit-sharing, we were able to attract excellent employees.

Lee Sol-pi from Seoul, who became my close friend, read Hidemaru Deguchi's book *In Search of Meaning*, and, impressed by its philosophy, translated it into Korean and had 2,000 copies printed. Lee's friend Kang

Hong-quo lost her husband in the Korean War and was the President of the National War Widows' Association. Her son Son Young-chol came to work for Swany Korea after graduating from Seoul University. After serving as President of Swany Korea, he went on to become CEO of Swany America, and since 2013 he has been enjoying retirement in Busan.

When recruiting, since we were in a country where I didn't speak the language, and to avoid any preferential treatment, I decided to try out a device for testing manual dexterity developed by the Ministry of Labour (a panel 30 cm × 20 cm × 3 cm in size with multiple holes in which pegs of assorted colours are inserted and turned). This aptitude test was highly effective since manual dexterity and patience are essential for this kind of work.

In 1976, we established Swany Orient at a site in the west of the country, and next door we established Swany Asia.

Following the example of Wells Lamont, the biggest manufacturer of work gloves in America with the most sophisticated production facilities, we aimed to have dedicated factories for each glove type. Thus, at Swany Korea, we produced cold-weather gloves of artificial leather and split cow leather; at Swany Orient we made artificial leather skiing gloves; and at Swany Asia we made all-leather gloves.

We recruited a workforce of about 400, which later grew to 650. The starting salary was ¥8,000. At the time, the average monthly wage in Japan was ¥30,000 to ¥40,000. About 70% of pay was taken up by performance incentives. The venture was a success, thanks to the eagerness of the Korean workers.

We eventually lost to China in price competition, however, and by 1990 we had closed all three factories and sold them to local businesses. In 1979, when South Korean President Park Chung-hee was assassinated, a strange atmosphere pervaded the factory, while outside there were clashes between demonstrators and the military, with nationalistic and anti-Japanese feelings coming to the surface in some places. However, the effect on business was not as great as media reports suggested.

'Runaway' accusation

With rising labour costs in Korea, we were not making money, and things reached a critical stage. Our final withdrawal came with the closure of Swany Asia in 1989. At the end of that year, five young women representing the union came to Japan, and I met them at Tokushima Airport. When I broached the subject of financial compensation, they jumped on me, saying 'We're here to defend the honour of the Korean people, not for money.'

Junior Executive Director Im, a Korean, had informed me that a group of female officials would be coming over to negotiate, and sensing that my guard was down, he warned me: 'In Korea, once a male worker is blacklisted, he finds it impossible to get new work, so men don't get involved in union activities that much. The really scary ones are the women, who have the option of getting married instead of looking for a new job.'

The Japanese newspapers seized on this, and printed headlines such as 'Labour-management talks on disengagement to extend into the new year', 'Runaway company chasing cheap labour', 'Unilaterally reneging on agreement', 'Scuffle with Korean union representatives', 'Refusal to negotiate', and the like. There were nearly a hundred such media reports. Over three months, we received more than 7,000 letters and postcards of protest from all over the country, saying things like 'President Miyoshi is evil,' 'Save the poor women!' and so on.

A journalist came from the Japanese newspaper *Asahi Shimbun*. 'You're disengaging now that you can no longer make a profit, aren't you?' I countered, 'If you saw two pairs of gloves exactly the same but one pair cost ¥1,500 and the other pair cost ¥2,500, which would you buy?' but my question wasn't answered. 'We provided work and contributed to the local economy for many years, but we couldn't win against Chinese competition. Please report the truth,' I appealed, but again I was ignored.

There were 19 sessions of talks extending over 100 days, including seven all-night negotiations. I had tape recorders and ashtrays thrown at me. 'Have you any idea what it was like for our country to be occupied for 36 years?' I was shouted at repeatedly. I clenched my teeth and endured it until morning.

CEO Son of Swany America, a Korean, encouraged me: 'You mustn't be so soft. You've done nothing to be ashamed of. The staff are free to leave if they want to, and you have the right to let the staff go provided you pay them a severance allowance. That's fair.' I decided to change my apologetic attitude.

March came, and still every Saturday and Sunday I found myself confronted by the union officials and about 400 of their supporters. I handed over a written statement saying that as they had requested, we would not pay a penny in compensation, and calling on them to stop their protests. A fight then broke out, which was brought under control by the police, but unfortunately there were injuries, including broken bones, on both sides. Not long afterwards, I received a telephone call from the union representatives. 'Mr Miyoshi, shall we talk about the money?'

Negotiations continued for two days and nights at a nearby hotel, and on 6 March we replied to the union's demand of ¥150,000,000, saying that ¥5,000,000 was our limit. 'Peanuts!' they said, which angered me.

Early in the morning of the second day, I cried out, 'Suit yourselves,' and went home and got into bed, but I couldn't sleep. In the end, the matter was settled with payment of compensation of ¥30,000,000.

Looking back, I think about the way we were characterised as a 'runaway company' and wonder what this meant. It seems to me that a company looking for a place where labour costs are low is a matter of self-defence in the struggle for survival. By transferring production, prices in the developed countries can be kept from rising, while bringing employment opportunities and improvement in quality of life to the developing countries. This seems to me the only way to make quality products available throughout the world at an affordable price. Nowadays all companies are doing it, and it's regarded as perfectly normal, but in those days, we were subjected to a lot of criticism, and as a representative of Swany, who were pioneers in this business practice, I feel that in a way I was made a scapegoat.

Swany America founded

In the 1970s, a number of major retail chains suggested that we maintain stocks in America, so that they could place extra orders when the weather got colder. In 1980, we established Swany America (SA), with Isamu Hasegawa as President and Tom Bridges, former buyer for Sears, as Vice President.

We rented 93 m² of office space on the 12th floor of the Empire State Building for $25,000 a year (about ¥5 million). The rent was comparable to rents in Tokyo. There were several glove companies nearby, so near in fact that we could dash out to see each other without an umbrella even when it rained, which was very convenient for us and our customers. We rented a warehouse in New Jersey for $50,000 (about ¥10 million) a year, and established our presence in America, feeling our way as we went.

With the expansion of our activities in America, we embarked on the development of new products for the American market. At just this time, the Pilot Ink Company, of fountain pen fame, introduced a new printing technology which produces colours when the temperature reaches 8°C or lower, and we used this technology to make children's gloves with appealing designs such as a peacock displaying its feathers, which appear when worn outside on a cold day. We called these gloves 'Freezy Freakies', or FF for short.

We spent $3 million (about ¥700 million) on TV advertising, and in nine years we sold two million pairs for $12 million (about ¥3 billion). Children's gloves that would normally be about $4 sold for $12, and our customers extended across the whole of the United States.

Richard, CEO of the top manufacturer Grandoe, congratulated me, saying, 'Etsuo, you've beaten us!' and told me this story. Apparently one of Grandoe's executives came home one day to find a pair of Freezy Freakies in the refrigerator. He asked his son 'What's wrong with our gloves?' to which the boy replied, 'I'd rather have gloves with pictures that appear in the cold!'

In 1987, we bought the long-established firm Elmer Little, who had been one of our customers. To gain a foothold in department stores, we paid about $385,000 (about ¥60 million) in royalties. We also took on all their stock, which caused us serious cash-flow problems, and we continued to have difficulties for about ten years, including having to cut staff. It was a valuable experience.

In 1989, we launched Swany's first American brand, 'Swany Ski'. We were sponsors of the United States speed skiing team and the World Cup and began exhibiting at the Snowsports Industries America Ski Show in Las Vegas.

Our Flexor brand is a glove with jointed fingers for dexterity, made using spin-off technology bought from NASA for $100,000 (about ¥20 million).

The Flexor Toaster is a mitten that can be zipped and unzipped while being worn, revealing a glove inside. Waterproof, breathable and warm, it has a lining of Triplex (a three-layer insulating material).

In this way, we became the first to have a glove with a price label of more than $100 a pair on the American market.

Swany China is born

While we were under pressure to take drastic measures to deal with the failing competitiveness of our three Korean companies in the face of Chinese competition, President Hiroshi Mino of our main bank, the Hyakujushi Bank, approached me and asked if we would be interested in expanding into China. A top executive from the Bank of China who was visiting Japan had approached him, asking him if he knew any glove companies, and the name of Miyoshi immediately sprang to his mind.

In February 1984, I went to China with Mr Mino and others. Shivering in the cold, we visited Hangzhou, Shanghai, Nanjing, Suzhou and Kunshan, and every day and every night we received a big welcome with much toasting. On our second visit in March, we focussed on Suzhou, and in April we settled on the city of Kunshan, situated between Suzhou and Shanghai. From then on, I spent one week there every month for talks with Xuan Binglong, the Director of the Kunshan Development Zone, and ten others.

With capital of $1.5 million (about ¥300 million), 52% from Japan and 48% from China, the land-use rights at an annual 5.5 yuan × 10,500 m² × 20 years, totalling 1.15 million yuan (about ¥100 million) would come from the Chinese side. The period of the joint venture was to be 20 years, and the monthly salary for the 400 staff, including insurance, pension, and other benefits, was to be 180 yuan (about ¥9,000), a level at which we could maintain competitiveness. The company name, however, proved to be a stumbling block.

I wanted the company name to be 'Swany China', but the Chinese side wanted 'China Swany'. I insisted on 'Swany China' since in our other locations the word 'Swany' had always come first. We negotiated all day, but the matter of the name was not settled, and the talks ground to a halt. Before dawn the next day, the idea came to me in a dream of making 'China Swany' the Chinese name and 'Swany China' the English name. After two days, we agreed on this as a fair solution.

The next sticking point was participation ratios. Three weeks of discussions ended in deadlock. I pushed for a 60% majority investment for the Japanese side, but the Chinese side would not concede on this. While the talks were going on, I visited the Japanese spinning company Toyoboshi, who were expanding into China. President Kobayashi told me that 'In China, connections are all-important, and it is essential to build relationships of trust.' On this advice, I decided that our side would give way, and we settled on a fifty-fifty Japan-China investment.

During the marathon negotiations, I visited China five times and spent 30 days in meetings, and we signed a 63-item agreement. Afterwards, our company participated in the Kunshan City Investment Fairs held in Osaka and Tokyo.

The following year, with the factory now ready, the day came for the grand opening. My wife Yoshiko made tea according to the Japanese tea ceremony, and ten of the female staff helped with the serving. Bank President and Ms Mino, Vice President Ling Zhiwei of the Bank of China and other guests tasted my wife's green tea while the media crowded round.

Yoshiko Miyoshi performs the Japanese tea
ceremony at the grand opening of Swany China,
1985

The event was a festival of Japanese culture, with 400 lunchboxes containing traditional Japanese delicacies such as herring wrapped in kelp, tea ceremony utensils weighing a total of 300 kg, and a commemorative planting of 50 cherry saplings. We kept the cost, including that of the banquet, to ¥300,000, in readiness for the disaster that might be awaiting us in this unfamiliar socialist country.

Sixteen years later, in 2001, the factory moved to a new 12,000 m² site on the corner of a major crossroads in the city centre, and in 2003, Swany acquired the Chinese capital for six million yuan (about ¥50 million).

The Japanese expansion into China began with Deng Xiaoping's request for help with modernisation of the electronics industry, and the response of Kōnosuke Matsushita, the founder of Panasonic. Among the major companies that expanded into China, Swany was the first foreign-owned enterprise in Jiangsu Province. However, in 2019, the number of employees had shrunk to one quarter, and Swany is now going forward with plans to move out of the city.

Crossing cultural barriers

Although a city of 500,000 inhabitants, Kunshan had a provincial feel, surrounded by rice fields. In 1984, I was the first foreigner to stay at the 'Kunshan Guest House'.

The room had a bath and a double bed, but the rug in the middle of the floor was soiled and covered in cigarette burns. The bathwater was muddy and rust-coloured, and you couldn't see the bottom of the tub. The price of the room was 15 yuan (about ¥2700) per night, but foreigners had to pay using 'foreign exchange certificates' (these could be used for buying imported goods and, on the black market, were worth 50% to 80% more than their face value).

There was no key, and no privacy. One morning, I was lying naked on my bed doing my Nishi-shiki gymnastics as usual (see Part 3) when, looking to my side, I was surprised to see one of the female staff was observing me.

The hotel boiler shut down at eight in the evening, and there was no hot water for bathing after parties. I got one of the staff to bring me ten pots of hot water from the kitchen. When I offered her a ¥1,000 note as a tip, she looked at it, turning it over and holding it up to the light, but didn't want to take it. When I showed her a dollar bill I found in my wallet, her face lit up as she accepted it. 'You use a lot of water, don't you,' she said, 'we only use one pot full for a wash.'

Mosquito-repellent incense was provided, but it was so smoky that I couldn't sleep, so instead of using it, I let the mosquitoes bite me, and while they were feeding on me, I slapped them with the palm of my hand one by one before sleeping. It was four or five years later that the 'Vape' electric mosquito repellent was made available.

Because of my history of polio, my feet get cold, and I used to carry an electric blanket and a 220V-100V transformer with me, but often this was made useless by night-time power cuts. Sometimes the whole town would suddenly lose its electricity. Power was supplied to seven districts according to the days of the week, and the day when it was our turn for a power cut was Swany's day off work.

Everyone out on the streets of the grey town wore 'Mao jackets', and none of the women wore make-up. Food, soap, fabrics, even matches were all rationed, and coupons were needed when buying them. The average area of a house in the city was 30 m², with shared toilet and shower (by 2017 this was 57 m² with toilet).

Breakfast at the guest house was a delicious meal of rice gruel and pickled Chinese mustard, with fried green vegetables and fried noodles. There were also *pidan*, fermented duck eggs, but I found the smell of these rather too pungent for me.

When I went to my favourite restaurant in town, I was greeted with a 'Welcome, welcome!' while the remains of the previous customer's meal were swept off the table. I always had the fried rice, which cost 1.5 yuan (about ¥60) and was very tasty and satisfying.

In the lobby on the upstairs floor of the guest house, I watched the Japanese TV drama *Oshin*, the story of a girl who grew up in the early years of the 20th century and the hardships she experienced throughout her life before eventually founding a successful supermarket business. I remember being there watching the episode where Oshin, played by the 10-year-old Ayako Kobayashi, is sent down the Mogami River on a raft to work as a servant in another village. At the time, few people in China had television, and the lobby of the guest house was heaving with about a hundred people from the neighbourhood who had come to watch, and I even worried that the floor might give way under their weight. *Oshin* was hugely popular in China as well as in Japan.

Confrontation

We started production at the Kunshan factory in February 1985, with a team of five headed by General Manager Tōru Mitsunaka sent over from Japan.

Seven months later, a report came that about a hundred workers were staging a go-slow, taking naps in the middle of the day. I flew out straight away, and arriving there I found a few dozen people lying on a pile of material, looking at me as if to say, 'Who are you?' I went straight to Director Xuan Binglong to discuss the situation, but the Director was adamant that they couldn't be dismissed. I persisted, 'Surely it says in the contract that dismissal is possible,' but I didn't get anywhere.

As a last resort, I asked my younger brother and Senior Executive Director Asao back at Headquarters to come over for a while to help out. It was a hard task, but he came out for the sake of saving the venture from collapse.

Straight away, we piled up pallets in the factory, and Asao got up and kept a lookout from a height of about one metre. This was successful in stopping the naps, but the workers were not putting all their energy into the job, just looking around. They all came to work by bicycle and crowded into the bicycle shed. They all left their bicycles by the entrance, so that the back of the bicycle shed was empty, while the entrance was blocked. Asao locked all the bicycles at the entrance and went back to his lodgings. Unable to go home, they gave in, and from the next morning they parked their bicycles in the back of the shed.

The work was not going well at all. I travelled to China every month and had meetings with Board Chairman Xuan of the Development Zone, but we made no progress. By and by, the year drew to an end, and the financial statement showed a large deficit. In January, the first board meeting was held, and together with General Manager Mitsunaka I prepared for a confrontation. Our opponents were the Board Chairman and about ten others from the Development Zone.

At the grand opening of Swany China. Left to right:
Mitsunaka, Xuan, Xu (interpreter), the author

My demands were in the immediate term to put the Japanese side in charge of management, to introduce a commission pay system, and to dismiss the 100 sleepers. The first two demands were settled in two days, but on the evening of the second day the talks reached deadlock on the issue of dismissals.

Board Chairman Xuan spoke. 'Here in China, we must follow Chinese common sense. Dismissals are out of the question,' he yelled, beating the table. I yelled back, 'You should know that your Chinese common sense is totally lacking in common sense!' Everyone went quiet. I had caused him to lose face, something the Chinese hate. We left the meeting, saying that we wanted to have a discussion among ourselves.

Several hours later the meeting resumed. The Chinese directors proposed a compromise, whereby only 50 staff would be dismissed. I rejected this. 'I don't want a single employee who doesn't work,' I said. After further discussion, another proposal came forward. 'What about 75, then?' This was what I had been waiting for.

A week passed by and still there was no improvement in efficiency. But I tolerated it. By the second week, a few of the staff started to work harder. They knew that their wages would increase by 20-30% because of the commission pay I had offered. Presently, they all suddenly started working seriously, and more than half of them turned up at seven o'clock although work didn't start until eight. They even started to run to the toilet for comfort breaks. After two years, we had recouped our losses. We had overcome the first great hurdle.

However, the wall of Board Chairman Xuan's house was daubed with death threats written in blood.

My brother's diary

My brother Asao kept a diary, which gives a good picture of life in Kunshan. Here are some extracts:

I was going to China for the first time in my life, and I left with a heavy heart. I didn't know the language, and I was lacking in confidence. I couldn't go over General Manager Mitsunaka's head, and if I had, he would probably have resigned. What was clear was that of three factories in Korea, one had closed down and the other two were in the red, and if we didn't succeed in China that would be the end for Swany.
In the newly built living quarters for the Japanese, rats walked across our faces while we were sleeping, and when we got up, we trod on insects scattered around our beds like so many black sesame seeds. We closed the net screens on the windows and put up mosquito nets, but the insects found a way in through the cracks. There were lumps of cement stuck to the inside of the bathtub, which tore into the skin on our backs.
Every day there was a strike at the factory, and nobody was paying any attention to instructions. If you told them to look right, they would look left. They would roll up the glove material and sleep on it, and when you scolded them, they would give you a weary look as they slowly got up. They started cleaning up at about half past three

and waited for the five o'clock bell while jabbering away to each other.

Mitsunaka was my junior at Waseda University, and I had worked with him since Korea. If the staff turned against me, I could simply go back to Japan, and I was determined to do what I could, even if it meant being disliked.

On Sunday, I invited Takahiro Tanaka and Hidenobu Mitani to cross the canal with our bicycles and go fishing. On the other side of the canal, one of the workers, Zhang Fengyi, offered us lunch, and we couldn't say no to her. The rice was cooked in water from the canal, and we felt very brave eating it, but it didn't give us any problems. On the way back she gave us a present of vegetables and half a dozen eggs.

Her mother was still young at 45 and had handsome features, but her face was dark and wrinkled. I was amazed at how working in the fields had aged her skin, and felt sorry for her, thinking of the hard life she had had.

The boat across the canal cost six *fen* (six hundredths of a yuan, about ¥2). Half a kilo of rice cost 15 *fen* (about ¥7), a bicycle cost 200 yuan (about ¥8,000), and a TV cost 100 yuan (about ¥4,000). Agricultural produce was cheap, while industrial products were expensive.

Breakthrough in Northeast China

After Swany China was established, every time I visited China I received an invitation from Wu Kequan, the County Governor of Kunshan. I asked him if he could introduce me to graduates who had studied Japanese at university. He agreed, but nothing happened. General Manager Mitsunaka had taken a crash course in Chinese at the Berlitz School but was far from being able to communicate adequately.

Three years later, I was with the County Governor, and while he had left his seat the interpreter told me, 'Only six people, 1% of county government employees, are university graduates.' I then asked about other districts where graduates in Japanese were employed. I found out that there was such a place, a city called Dongguan, just north of Hong Kong, and I decided to go there straight away.

I visited factories making socks, dies, and toys, and learned that in each company there were several senior staff who spoke Japanese. The boss told me, 'If we advertise in the national papers, we get many applicants from the three northeast provinces.' They arrived after a train journey lasting a whole week. This was because in Harbin, the capital of Heilongjiang Province, there were four universities with Japanese departments, but there were no Japanese companies there.

Astonished to hear this vital piece of information, I went straight to the airport and joined a long queue for tickets, bought myself a one-way ticket to Harbin and flew out to the northeast via Shanghai. At the airport there were only four taxis. I won the bidding for a taxi and took off, hiring the car for 350 yuan for the day (about ¥14,000). The dilapidated taxi had a hole in the floor that I could see the road through, and the door rattled if I didn't pull on it.

I visited Harbin Institute of Technology, Harbin Medical University, Harbin University of Science and Technology and Harbin Normal University without any appointment. All four institutions were surprised at my visit, and said it was the first time they had been approached by a Japanese employer. In the staff room, I showed them the terms we were offering: a monthly salary of 700 yuan (about ¥27,000) with accommodation and other benefits provided. The Japanese department heads listened eagerly. One whispered in my ear so as not to be overheard, 'Never mind the students, have you got a job for me?'

I invited Department Head Jin of the Harbin Institute of Technology to dinner, and gently turned down his request for a job, explaining that three years' probation on the factory floor was essential. Much to my delight, however, he kindly accompanied me to the Heilongjiang newspaper offices, and helped me place a B5-size advertisement translated into Chinese.

The advertisement had a massive impact: in two months, we received 55 applications for jobs at Swany China. We fixed a date and time for the interviews, which would be held at Harbin International Hotel.

I visited China again, and as a result of the interviews, we hired Gao Zhangfeng from Harbin Normal University, who was proficient in Chinese, Japanese, Korean and English, and we carried out background checks on another 21 interviewees. Two months later, we received a valuable report from Gao on the other applicants.

This was the former Manchuria, where, at the end of World War II, countless Japanese colonists had fled, giving rise to the tragedy of the Japanese orphans left behind after the war. Why was there such an interest in learning the Japanese language in this part of China, which had been invaded and occupied by Japan?

I returned in March, armed with Gao's report. I wound my way past piles of frozen rubbish to the apartment of Huang Yubin of the Harbin Institute of Technology. There was a bathtub just big enough to sit in up to one's waist in the living room, and Huang told me that he bathed in this tub, boiling a potful of water, and mixing it with cold.

Zhang Taifu of the Normal University had wrapped the door of his house in cloth to keep out the draught. His reason for applying was our offer to provide accommodation.

In this freezing cold city with temperatures of -30 degrees, we invited seven people to the hotel for interviews. As a result, in addition to Gao, our first recruit, we decided to hire five people: Zhang Taifu, Kong Shitai of the University of Science and Technology, Jin Dehua of Mudanjiang Normal University, Huang Yubin of Harbin Institute of Technology, and his wife, of the Normal University.

When they arrived at Kunshan, where Swany China was, the first thing they asked was to be allowed to lie down. After travelling for 40 hours in the 'hard seat' (second class) carriage, they were feeling faint and dizzy, and couldn't sit up any longer.

The new recruits didn't settle in easily. Huang went on to become General Manager of Swany China, but after 12 years he moved to Canada with his family. Communication improved, but eventually all the university graduates from the northeast left, having served only in a transitional role. At present, the senior positions are held by local staff.

With the continuing boom in investment in China, candidates for executive positions left for Japanese light electric companies. Perhaps this was just a sign of changing times, perhaps they were anxious about the future of a company selling a seasonal product – or were they worried about my managerial ability?

Focus on China

In 1988, when Swany China was getting off the ground, I made an unannounced visit to the county government in Jiashan County, Zhejiang Province, about one and a half hours by car to the west, together with Gao. I wanted to compare investment conditions in Jiangsu and Zhejiang Provinces. We received a warm welcome, and after three days of talks, a joint venture with a local glove factory was decided upon, and 'Swany Great Wall' (GW) was established, with capital of $1,150,000 (about ¥130 million), the Japanese side owning 51%.

Chu Byong-su from Korea took on the role of General Manager. The average wage is 4,200 yuan (about ¥60,000), with performance incentives taking up 53%. At one time there were 400 staff; now only half that number remain, but GW continues to produce 2.1 million pairs of fabric and artificial leather gloves a year, generating a 10% profit.

Supervisor Eiji Hayase wrote in the 2018 GW report, 'In the industry, digitisation of feed control, thread tension control and pressure adjustment of Juki sewing machines is proceeding. At GW, however, we still use lockstitch machines, and yet our workers can sew small parts at an amazing speed, as if operator and machine have become one. It's most impressive to see.'

In the same year, 1988, we rented 10,000 m² of land about two kilometres south of Swany China in Kunshan and established 'Swany Glove' with Japanese capital of $1,350,000. Kim Hyang-jun, also from Korea, became General Manager, and Jin Dehua from Harbin became Assistant General Manager. At one time there were 400 staff, but in 2010 there were only half this number, making fabric and leather gloves and golf gloves, and now the factory has closed.

In 1989, in a joint venture with a local company, we established 'Swany Taicang' (TG) in Taicang, Jiangsu Province. Shu Jinzhu became General Manager. After that, we bought the Chinese capital, making it a wholly Japanese-owned company. The number of staff has gone down from 320 to 170 and is planned to go down further to 130 in five years' time. Yearly output is 1.3 million pairs.

A high proportion of TG's production was outsourced, and waste leather gloves, sewn from leather sorted at the employees' homes, are also made here. We pursued high-mix low-volume production to the limit, but we still struggle to stay profitable.

In 2006, we established the Swany China Qingyang Factory in Anhui Province. Unable to recruit the 400 staff originally planned, the factory started with 150 staff and now has 103. The cost of this oversized factory is currently a heavy burden for us.

China, an economic superpower

The following is a report on conditions in modern China, from General Manager Tu Zhengdong of Swany China writing in *Swany News*:

One Sunday in 2019, a friend and his wife came and said, 'Let's go to Beijing for National Day.' I turned down their suggestion, saying that I had been the previous year on the company trip. 'In that case, we'll go just the two of us,' they said, and immediately booked seats on the high-speed train and four nights' hotel accommodation by smartphone, paying 4,800 yuan (about ¥72,000).

At 8.30 this morning, my wife ordered some salt and milk from the supermarket RT-Mart, paying 53 yuan (about ¥800) by Alipay, and the goods were delivered at 10.30. She also recently ordered some cookware costing 388 yuan (about ¥6,000) on the online shopping site Taobao, and the goods were delivered the next day. Shopping costing 39 yuan (about ¥600) or more is delivered free of charge. Grocery bills, power bills, even taxi fares can be paid by smartphone.

In the old days, the train to Shanghai, about 65 kilometres east of Kunshan, took an hour, but now the high-speed train takes you there in just 18 minutes. Many Shanghai people have moved out to Kunshan and commute to Shanghai by rail.

More than 90% of people live in newly built apartments, and own real estate. School education from the first year of elementary school to the third year of junior high school is free, and insurance covers 80% of healthcare costs for working people, and 90% for the retired. So, 40 years on from China's economic reforms, rapid development has been achieved. China is joining the ranks of economic superpowers like the United States and Japan and receiving the attention of the world. It is still developing, but the future China will surely be an economic superpower worthy of the name.

Anti-Japanese demonstrations

Going back some years to 2012, when Sino-Japanese relations were strained over the sovereignty of the Senkaku (Diaoyu) Islands, General Manager Mitsunaka writes in *Swany News*:

I regularly go to eat at a Japanese restaurant called Ajisato in central Kunshan. There are several Japanese bars, canteens, and noodle shops nearby, and on 15 September these were attacked by a mob of angry young people, who smashed their signboards before forcing their way in to cause further damage, something that had never been heard of before. The manager of Ajisato had the presence of mind to display a Chinese flag in the entrance to her establishment and seems to have avoided any damage.

All the Japanese shops in the city stayed closed, and the police advised Japanese residents to stay indoors. All we could do was lie low, avoiding going out, and keep an eye on the situation. At the Toyota showroom next door, a dozen or so cars were battered and overturned. As a Japanese who has been associated with China for nearly 30 years, these events fill me with great sadness.

What first sparked off the trouble was the announcement by Tokyo Governor Shintarō Ishihara that the Tokyo Metropolis would buy the Senkaku Islands. He has kept quiet since the trouble started, but I'd like to hear how he feels about it now. Since 13 September there has been a notice outside the Kunshan Tax Office saying, 'No dogs or Japanese'. I sincerely hope that the Chinese side adopts a calm, grown-up response to this situation.

Breaking into the Chinese market

In 1993, together with Gao, I travelled to Beijing and to the northeastern cities of Shenyang, Changchun, and Harbin.

In Beijing, I had my first meeting with a buyer at the glove section of the Beijing Department Store in Wangfujing Street. She showed an interest in our sheepskin and pigskin men's and ladies' gloves and luxury children's mittens. 'You're the first salesperson we've had from Japan,' she said. 'Thank you for coming.' We received orders for 800 pairs. In Beijing we visited six retailers, including Xirong Shopping Centre and Baode Shopping Centre.

In one week, we visited 21 department stores in four cities, and we received orders from half of these, totalling 12,000 pairs. At 30%, our profit margin was small (in other countries this would typically be about 40-60%), but a bigger problem was getting paid.

We took the train from Beijing to Shenyang in Liaoning Province. We had to queue for an hour and a half to buy our tickets, and the six o'clock train was so packed that it was impossible to go to the toilet. I gave the conductor 10 yuan (about ¥160) and she let me use her bed, 'but only as far as Shenyang'. We arrived at 11 o'clock at night. In Shenyang, we visited five retailers including Shenyang Shangyecheng, strong on quality brands, and Xiwu Baihuo, with a reputation for service. Even now, old administrative and commercial buildings from the Japanese colonial period remain and are being given a new life, and the city as a whole is a living museum of historical heritage.

Our next stop was Changchun in Jilin Province. Gao resorted to jumping the long queue at the ticket office and emerged with our tickets. But when we boarded the train, we found it was standing room only, and packed. We squeezed our way through to the first-class carriage. Gao started asking the passengers, 'Please give your ticket to a disabled Japanese man. We'll pay you three times the price of the ticket!' The fifth passenger he asked agreed to exchange tickets with me, and I was finally able to sit down. In Changchun, we visited five retailers including Baihuo Dalou and Guoji Maoyi.

Our last destination was Harbin, 300 kilometres north of Changchun. This was my fourth visit. Gao very assertively managed to get a seat for me on the train. We visited five retailers including Hualian and Qiulin. At the time, both were thriving department stores, but in recent years they have been struggling against competition from online shopping sites such as Taobao and Xiaomi.

The city was built by the Russian Empire and has a European appearance, with cobblestone streets, Russian Orthodox churches, and acacia-lined avenues, and has been called 'the Paris of the Orient'. Japan was also involved in Harbin's history. The city was the scene of the assassination in 1909 of Itō Hirobumi, the Japanese Resident General of Korea. It was also in Harbin that horrific human experiments were carried out by the notorious Unit 731, the Japanese Imperial Army's secret biological warfare research facility, during World War II.

I bought a lunch box at the station for 2.5 yuan (about ¥40) but found it hard to eat. The stewed bell peppers had a suspiciously sour taste, and the rest consisted of rice with a few peanuts and some powdered squid scattered on top. I made myself eat it, although it was like chewing on sand. I found three small stones – it seemed that they didn't have the machines for removing stones from rice. Takahiro Tanaka, a Japanese colleague who came to work at Swany China, actually broke one of his front teeth on a stone.

As I mentioned above, the profit margin was about half that in Western countries, and the retailers operate on a commission basis, making it a very difficult market. The fact that the labour costs of local Chinese companies were about a fifth of the Japanese meant that we couldn't be competitive, and, as I also mentioned above, there were problems in collecting payments. In the end, after a second sales trip, I decided we should give up trying to sell on the domestic Chinese market.

Into Southeast Asia

In rapidly developing China, holding on to staff is not easy, and in 2011 we started production in Cambodia, establishing 'Swany Cambodia' in the Tai Seng Bavet Special Economic Zone, about two hours by road from Ho Chi Minh City across the border in Vietnam. With capital of $3 million (about ¥300 million) Swany Cambodia began producing fabric gloves with a workforce of 300.

The staff are paid an average of $192 (about ¥20,000) with performance incentives, in addition to which they also receive overtime pay, attendance allowances and travelling expenses. The number of staff receiving performance incentives in excess of fixed salary is low at 10%, compared with 90% in China, which is a problem. The first President was Sakuji Imataki, who has passed the baton to the new President, Yasushi Okudai.

Cambodia borders Thailand to the west, Vietnam to the east and Laos to the north. About 15 million people live in an area about 80% of the main island of Japan. The language spoken is Khmer, said by some to be the hardest language in the world to learn.

Having to arrange transport for staff from different neighbourhoods, a fiendishly difficult language, productivity at least 20% lower than elsewhere, having to procure materials via Vietnam, slow and expensive transport, all these meant that it took eight years before we finally broke even. The increase in productivity, in spite of the coronavirus pandemic, has been a windfall.

The need to provide transport for the staff makes offering overtime difficult. The pronunciation and grammar of Khmer are both hard to master, and other Japanese companies have adopted the solution of teaching the local staff Japanese. To give an example, the Cambodians count one to five as we do, but six is five plus one, seven is five plus two, and so on, which causes confusion. Productivity is impeded by the many public holidays: 23 a year.

At one time, the brutal policies of the Pol Pot government led to the deaths of an estimated three million people through starvation and tor ture, but with the return of peace following this dark period, the country has set out to achieve economic recovery and self-reliance.

Meanwhile, we have also invested $500,000 in the Vietnam factory of the Taiwanese company Well Mart, where we are making fabric, artificial leather, and real leather skiing gloves. There are 430 employees, and the average monthly wage is about $300 (about ¥30,000), with additional performance incentives. Apart from the lunar new year, there are only five public holidays a year. The people are skilled and hardworking, and quality is high. Deputy Manager Kenji Okumura is currently in charge of production and quality control.

We also outsource to Indonesia, where there is a young workforce, and shipment to Japan takes no more than two weeks. Products made here include golf, batting, fishing, and skiing gloves.

6. Breakthrough

Trusting in the young

We sent Tōru Mitsunaka, who had graduated from Waseda University in 1979, to work at Swany Korea for three and a half years, after which we sent him to JAIMS, Fujitsu's management training institute in Hawaii, for six months. After this, he took up duties as Swany China's first general manager at the age of 27. His great efforts there were reflected in the company's success. His experience in dealing with difficult situations was invaluable in leading this great family of 400 people.

In 1988, I established Swany Great Wall in Jiashan County, Zhejiang Province, near Shanghai. The following year, General Manager Mitsunaka started negotiations with the executives of Kunshan City in Jiangsu Province, and launched Swany Glove, the first wholly Japanese-owned enterprise in the province. The new company came into being with just a signature from me. And in 1990, Swany Taicang was established in Taicang, also near Shanghai, this time Mitsunaka signing as my representative.

He took charge of materials, personnel and management for the four Chinese companies, and since 2015 he has been resident in Cambodia.

Chu Byong-su was 35 when he took on the role of General Manager of Swany Great Wall, and Shu Jinzhu was 33 when he began service as General Manager of Swany Taicang. Isamu Hasegawa was 27 when he became CEO of Swany America.

These young men took responsibility for the management of our subsidiaries at an age unimaginable in most companies. While on the one hand it might seem risky to appoint such young people, I thought that once they had taken up their posts, they would soon develop their strengths.

Swany trained up these young men by appointing them to important posts, but the truth was that there were no others we could have trusted more.

My successors

In 1992, my youngest daughter Yasuko brought her boyfriend home. His name was Tsukasa Itano, and she had got to know him at the trading company Naka Shoji in Takamatsu, where she was working. Believing that as parents we couldn't stand in the way of our daughter's wishes, Yoshiko and I gave them our blessing.

At Naka Shoji, Itano told us, he had applied himself to learning about the kimono business, and after some years he had gained experience in management. He told us that he had learned the importance of such Japanese concepts as resourcefulness and frugality, as popularised in the writings of the 17th-century Japanese author Ihara Saikaku.

On the many subsequent occasions when I met him, I sensed that he had a passion for business and a good grasp of the market, and I invited him to come and work at Swany as a potential successor. He joined the company in 1993 and went to work first at Swany China, and then the following year in the fashion division. In 2000 he became supervisor, then in 2004 divisional manager, and then in 2007 junior executive director. In 2009 he took office as President, and the baton passed to him.

Gathering to mark the changeover of president of Swany
(fourth from left: the author, fifth from left: President Itano,
sixth from right: Executive Director Kawakita), 2009

The company's onward march continued. In 2019, we worked on quality American style casual gloves, and at the Man Show in Paris our booth was especially busy. Buyers from European department stores praised our gloves, and sales to Japanese department stores also increased. Fumi Ueda, who has been with us for five years, is taking the lead in recruitment with an eye on the future, and a recruitment team of six people with an average age of 30 take the graduates by the hand and let them meet the employees so that they can experience the 'heart of Swany'. The results are positive.

The personnel appraisal system with emphasis on degree of contribution, the 'refresh leave' system which pays ¥50,000 when an employee takes paid leave, and support for 12 hobby circles including light music, golf and fishing are currently being promoted. Then there is the 'personal development support scheme', which helps with online English conversation, computers, and bookkeeping.

The aim is to achieve 'personal growth and success in life' through work, by connecting the values of the individual and the organisation. But what brings about true customer satisfaction is, needless to say, the motivation of the whole workforce.

Next process as customer

The idea of 'thinking of the next process as the customer' means working with the next process in mind, striving to make the next step easier at each stage in production. In everyday life, it's like leaving the bathroom clean for the next user. For me, travelling around the world selling Swany gloves, it meant thinking about the next step when making decisions in negotiations with customers.

Long ago, when Milton of Avon Glove wanted me to bring our price down, I got him to change the content of a dozen-pair set from two pairs of S, four pairs of M, four pairs of L and two pairs of XL to six pairs of M and six pairs of XL and agreed to a price reduction of 1%. This became the accepted combination, and for many years resulted in an improvement in productivity that more than compensated for the slight increase in the quantity of materials used.

There are many variables to consider in the manufacture of gloves, including such things as the stretchability of the material, the complexity of the decoration, the way of stitching the gloves together and sewing around the cuffs, the flexibility of the rubber, the overall shape, and so on. I was thinking about productivity almost as much as I was about winning orders.

At Swany China we had a very difficult job making 691 pairs for a certain customer with studs and a printed pattern on the back. The sewing had to be done very carefully so as not to spoil the printing, slowing the process down, and efficiency fell to one-third.

At Swany Great Wall, we had a struggle with 30 or 40 thousand pairs of artificial leather gloves for another customer. There were 30 kinds, in five colours and five sizes. For each kind, 17 dies were needed. Although low-priced, demand for quality was high, and the contractors found them very troublesome. We also needed price tags, size tags and material and quality labels, which added further to the work.

At Swany Taicang, we had another demanding job with the 100,000 pairs of gloves per year we made from waste leather. We needed to sort the leather according to oil content, colour, and size, matching left to right by colour, and the number of pieces obtained went down to one-third. Sewing was sometimes interrupted when tough leather had to be softened by beating it with hammers. It's hard to imagine this happening nowadays, but to save us from going into the red, the staff even took work home with them, without extra payment.

Indeed, whether we make a profit or whether we struggle is determined at the time of negotiating with customers. Stretchability of material varies infinitely, and a slight error in decorative sewing can bring about chaos throughout the factory. Along with all this, demand for compliance with wide-ranging regulations is becoming stricter year by year.

Most factory crises stem from arrangements made at the time of receiving orders. In the workplace, it is not easy to speak frankly to a sales executive who is one's superior. Junior Executive Director Hiroyoshi Iwazawa, who left the company in 2004 while still young, to care for his wife, said when leaving that the people at Headquarters lacked understanding of the problems faced by the factory staff, words that I shall always take to heart.

Swimming 250 metres a day

When I had just started doing business with Dorfman in San Francisco, I was in the airport hotel, unable to sleep because of jet lag. I had wrapped the telephone in a blanket so as not to be disturbed in the night and had just managed to get off to sleep when I heard someone knocking on the door of my room. There at the door was CEO Hyman, telling me it was already ten o'clock in the morning. I have a vivid memory of his commending the virtues of swimming as the most effective form of rehabilitation for people with polio.

Mr Chiodi in Italy had said the same thing, and so on returning to Japan I took up swimming in the sea at the back of our house.

I made marks on the two-metre-high sea wall in white paint every 50 metres, and between May and November I swam 150 metres along the coast to the west and back again. Nothing could compare with the exhilarating feeling after swimming.

In May the water was icy cold, but I endured it for the sake of building up my strength. The water gradually got more comfortable as the months passed, reaching its warmest in September. Even October was surprisingly warm, and, as I learned, the water in November was still mild compared with May. Swimming in the sea was not without its dangers, however. Because of the weakness in my right leg, the only stroke I can do is crawl. Not looking ahead while swimming, I once collided with a large piece of wood with a nail in it, which seriously injured my shoulder joint.

For safety's sake, I spent ¥1,500,000 on having a swimming pool built. On the site of the old factory on the south side of our house, I installed a pool 1.5 metres wide, 1 metre deep and 12.5 metres long, enclosed in glass. I went to my pool at seven o'clock every morning, and swam ten lengths each way, making 250 metres. The time actually spent swimming was 15 minutes but including drying, straightening my hair, and getting dressed it took half an hour.

I kept up swimming for 14 years, until I switched to Nishi-shiki gymnastics. During that time, I attempted 1,500 metres (60 lengths each way) three times. Testing myself to the limit of my endurance, I was gasping for breath at the end of it. After swimming, I had to lie down for a while to recover. But thanks to my efforts to overcome my disability, and despite having post-polio syndrome, I can still walk, with a Swany Bag in each hand for support, at the age of 81. How much longer I'll be able to walk I don't know, but I'm ever thankful for having above-average strength in my arms.

The Japanese athlete Hironoshin Furuhashi swam 1,500 metres in 18 minutes 19 seconds at the 1949 US Championships, and this achievement earned him the nickname 'the flying fish of Fujiyama'. This was about five times as fast as the 90 minutes I managed. My inability to swim faster was due to my weak right leg, although my strong arms compensated considerably.

Whirlwind of bankruptcies

When I was still very young, our customer Ichiba Shoji went bankrupt, and a meeting of about 20 creditors was held at our house. At one point the boss of one company, the biggest creditor, took a Japanese sword and put it in front of the President of Ichiba Shoji. 'Take this and die!' he said. Seeing the poor man grovelling in tears and begging for his life, I was horrified. I could literally feel my scrotum shrinking. For a businessperson, nothing could be crueller than bankruptcy.

In 1975, the year we transferred production to Korea, we were searching for other work in Japan. The trading company Nichimen suggested a business in ten-pin bowling, which was enjoying a 'boom' at the time. This was when my father was President. He bought 1,500 *tsubo* (about 5,000 m²) of land in Wakimachi, Tokushima Prefecture, and invested more than ¥300 million in a bowling alley which opened as 'Swany Wakimachi'.

The bowling alley was full of customers every day, and my father was ecstatic. He then tried to repeat this success with a second bowling alley in Ōchi, the neighbouring town. Business suddenly slumped, and he was lucky to be able to sell the premises to a supermarket, breaking even on the deal.

In the end, my father managed to dispose of 'Swany Wakimachi' too, selling it off to a local supermarket, but he came dangerously close to disaster.

My eldest brother said that the chances of success would be greater if we stuck to projects closely related to our main business, and he was right. My father went after a completely unrelated line of business, but fortunately he managed to avert catastrophe.

In 1997, a debt renegotiation attempt by our customer 'S' Bussan triggered a process which ended in the bankruptcy of several glove manufacturers including company 'T', company 'S' and company 'U'. Swany, too, incurred debts of nearly ¥300 million due to my own indecisiveness. Around this time, a whirlwind of bankruptcies swept through the whole industry, with about half of all glove companies going under.

In 2004, we established 'Swany Europe' to sell Swany's skiing gloves. Having to rely on local people may have been partly to blame, but in any case, we eventually had to withdraw in 2011 after suffering losses of nearly ¥200 million. Our vision for this new enterprise had been overoptimistic.

In 2003, following its success in Japan, we started selling the Swany Bag in the United States. The with-seat model was featured in an article in the New York Times, and it was also taken up by the TV shopping channel QVC. Unfortunately, it was not shown to its best advantage, its main function, that of a walking aid, not being adequately explained. In 2013 we withdrew from the market, having lost $1 million (about ¥100 million). We had failed to establish a culture of body-supporting luggage for people with leg problems.

Things had looked so promising, with Mr Graf in Boston writing to me congratulating me on appearing in the New York Times... It was a bitter disappointment.

It was Osamu Suzuki, Chairman of Suzuki Motor Corporation, who said that '50% failure and 50% success is normal. A businessperson should work to make the success 51% or more.'

Frankly, it sometimes seems a miracle to me that Swany, with all these failures under its belt, has come through as one of the 60 or so companies to survive out of the 230 glove manufacturers that once existed.

Postcard writing on days off

I can't drink alcohol, and as a result I'm sometimes called unsociable. To compensate, I took up writing postcards. I once attended a seminar given by the business consultant Yukio Funai, in which he said, 'If you send postcards three times, I can guarantee you'll succeed in getting orders.'

In an effort to try to keep the factories moving during the quiet season, I stayed in New York throughout July every year. On Saturdays and Sundays, I would set to work writing postcards, 50 in the morning and another 50 in the afternoon. By evening my right hand would be aching.

Picture postcards sold in books of 10 or 20 were good value. Once, in Poland, I bought every card in the shop, about 2,000 of them, and it cost me only about ¥8,000. In Cambodia picture postcards were only ¥3 each, so I bought a few thousand there, too. I also picked up 50 or 100 of the postcards given away by airlines. I would then send these from New York,

Toronto, or Helsinki. Perhaps I wrote about 600 a year. Since turning 80, I have cut this down to about 100.

Regrettably, a few of my friends mistakenly think this means I've got money to burn. I have to know at least something about the recipient before I can start writing, and it takes a serious attitude to keep it up. Assuming ¥100 for each card, that means ¥10,000 in one day. My leisure activities are listening to audio books and postcard-writing, which cost just pennies compared with expensive hobbies like golf, gambling, and night-time entertainment.

In 1995, I decided to buy a strip of public land about a metre wide between our company building and the four houses to the west. I was told that getting consent from more than one would be next to impossible, but as well as visiting them in person I sent postcards from China and Germany, and eight months later I obtained consent from all four. I also sent many postcards to my contact at the local Finance Bureau, and after a few months I obtained permission to purchase the land. The estate agent was very impressed, and asked me 'Have you got friends in the Finance Bureau?'

My postcard-writing had a big response. I had many messages from people thanking me for a card I had sent from Germany or somewhere.

I like to write personally in reply to the questionnaire postcards we receive from Swany Bag customers. I then get replies back from the customers, surprised to receive a card from me. Several times I have even been offered invitations to dinner by ladies, saying, 'If you ever come to Tokyo, please come and have dinner with me,' which makes me very happy.

If I send a card to someone who is in hospital it gets passed around the ward and read by the other patients, and I then hear from friends of friends 'I read your postcard to so-and-so.' It gives great pleasure to be thanked by so many people and to think I might have cheered someone up. I did, however, once get a response from an old classmate asking me 'not to write in difficult characters that I can't read'.

I once received a reply from a member of Japan Air Lines cabin crew I'd sent a card to.

'I noticed you had an unusual bag on the flight to Hong Kong and spoke to you. I'm still a novice only one year into the job. I was so happy to receive your card in the New Year. It was very encouraging. I do hope I can meet you again somewhere. Please take care!'

In this digital age that places efficiency above all else, it seems that people still crave the warmth of this old-fashioned, 'analogue' means of communication.

Simplification, specialisation, standardisation

Manufacturing industry is said to be basically 'moving things from one place to another', and the rationalisation of logistics is vital.

In the 1970s, when the company was using a mixture of B5 and A4 sizes of paper, I heard from Hiroyoshi Iwazawa, one of our directors, that Honda had made A4 their standard paper size, and I decided that we too should make A4 the standard for all our documents.

In 1972, when we moved operations to Korea, we made plastic boxes to hold 20 pairs of gloves that could be stacked high and stopped the practice of making bundles of 50 to 60 pairs tied with string, which could not be stacked. We stacked 3 × 4 boxes five tiers high onto a pallet, so that one person could then move 1,200 pairs at a time using a manual pallet jack. Materials in cartons were loaded onto pallets, and rolls of cloth were stored in a container 1 m wide × 1.3 m high × 1.5 m deep.

Boxes containing parts were loaded on to the top tier of a sloping roller conveyor and fed down, where they were taken by the sewing people. After sewing, they were placed on the lower tier and fed back. Fourchette fitting, stitching and other steps were carried out by specialised workers. This specialisation meant that skills that together would take several years to learn could be mastered in a matter of months. The idea for the method our 1,200 Korean factory staff were trained in came to me in a dream.

In 1982, we built an automated warehouse which allowed us to move goods in and out in about two minutes. There were 32 pallets arranged in four rows, stacked seven tiers high, giving a total of 896. However, in 2002, Masaru Yamada, the President of Shoei, who was advising us at the time, pointed out to us that the new warehouse makes it difficult to perform a visual inventory check. This is an important challenge yet to be resolved.

In 1985, we adopted the American Pantone colour system, so that we could indicate the colours of face, lining, stitching, tags and so on by numbers. This simplified things enormously.

In 2008, the production of A4 plastic files with 30 holes was discontinued, and we changed our files to the two-hole type, but at a subsequent management meeting this change was opposed as they were found to be harder to use, and so we reconsidered.

Putting a sheet of paper with two holes into a folder and taking it out again took 50 seconds, but with 30 holes it took only 26 seconds. With two holes, a bulging pile of filed documents had to be pressed down while reading or annotating. Moreover, the 30-hole paper had holes no more than one centimetre from the edge, leaving 20% more area on the page for typing. There were several thousand of these 30-hole folders still on sale, and so we went back to using them.

My successor as President, Tsukasa Itano, initiated a new filing system in 2020. Instead of fastening documents in folders, he has them put in small boxes. This, he says, has the twin benefits of being efficient and environmentally friendly. He is now embarked on a new programme of rationalisation, aimed at increased sharing of documents, easier searching, and reduced number of copies. If he succeeds, this will be introduced across the group.

Simplification, specialisation and standardisation in all things are crucial for survival.

Walking with a leg brace

Ever since I was born, I have been unable to walk long distances because my right ankle is unsteady. After starting junior high school, my physical activity increased, and, on the advice of my doctor, I started using a leg brace from below my knee to my toe joints, which enabled me to walk with ease. This brace is an expensive item, costing ¥60,000-¥70,000, and needs to be replaced every ten years, but the state subsidises it by 90%.

My first brace consisted of leather straps lined with artificial leather on a base of plastic with steel struts. If the inner surface came away from the skin surface even by a millimetre, it was painful and caused peeling and inflammation of the skin. Repeated fine adjustment was needed before it was satisfactory.

I am forever indebted to my technician, Toshiji Tsujimoto of Takamatsu Prosthetic Laboratories. The technician has to know the quirks of my leg inside out in order for the brace to work satisfactorily, and I am lucky to have had Mr Tsujimoto looking after me since my youth.

I wear a thin sock on my right foot and fit the brace on, and over this I wear a pair of socks on both feet. Because it used to contain metal, I was always stopped at the boarding gate at airports, but metal is no longer used, and I don't have this problem now. I still have a feeling of pressure when wearing it, however.

Travelling with a disability I

Usually when I travel, I go on the first morning flight, and so at six o'clock I leave for Tokushima Airport in my Toyota Prius. If I'm going abroad, I leave at five o'clock and take the Takamatsu Expressway bus from Ōchi to the airport. Getting up in the early morning is hard, but I get to meet people in the glove business, and it's a chance to exchange information.

I once visited the headquarters of K-Mart in Detroit at half past seven in the morning. The vast entrance was deadly quiet. As I pushed the door open, I wondered if I had timed my arrival a bit too early, but I was greeted with a smile and a 'Good morning!' Thousands of staff were already working. Apparently, they finish work at half past four in the afternoon.

Usually, when visiting Europe or America, I flew out on a Saturday or Sunday, did my selling from Monday to Friday, and returned to Japan after two or three weeks. If I was away for two weeks, I spent about ¥350,000, visiting 20 companies in 10 days at a cost of ¥18,000 per company. If I could only make it to 10 companies the cost went up to ¥35,000, and if adding wages these figures would be doubled.

Once, while I was watching television, a buyer from the department store Tokyu Hands appeared on the screen, and said that he made an average of 4.2 visits per day while travelling abroad. I was stunned to hear that he visited 20 or more companies in five days.

From 1996, when I embarked on the development of the Swany Bag, I flew every month to Taipei or Shanghai. I met with luggage and parts manufacturers at airport restaurants for about an hour and a half before flying straight home. On board the plane home, one of the JAL cabin crew once said to me, 'You were on this morning's flight, weren't you? You're having a busy day.' I got home a little after nine o'clock at night. The time I was on the move I spent reading. The things I took with me were as follows:

Razor, toothbrush, comb, 35 mm-diameter plastic bottle containing hair gel, ointment, soap, sewing set and document seal in a bag measuring 18 cm × 13 cm. I don't take any medicines. These items are still in my Swany Bag now and accompany me wherever I go. When I was at home, I also kept my wallet inside it, so that I didn't keep delivery people waiting.

Four or five books, clothes, pouch wrapped in a *furoshiki* cloth wrapper, placed in the bottom of a suitcase with 75 mm wheels. On top of this I laid out 100 to 150 single glove samples. This would come to about 20 kg. More often than not I would go straight from the airport to the customer, and the wrapping cloth served as a handy screen for my personal things. The *furoshiki* is a truly admirable product of Japanese culture.

I would wear the same navy blue suit every day and take just one shirt and tie and one spare pair of socks. I washed my underwear in the bath. If I wrapped it in a bath towel and gave it a good wring, it would usually be dry by morning. Very occasionally it would still be damp, but I hardly noticed, and in a short while the warmth of my body had dried it out.

On one occasion, as I was passing some people working with asphalt, a piece flew my way and got stuck to my shirt. I went back to the hotel and spent ten minutes frantically sucking at it and spitting out the dirt. I was relieved to see that the stain had nearly completely disappeared.

An annoyance for me was the different voltages and different socket shapes in different countries. I bought ones for Britain, Germany, France, and Italy and carried them around with me for 20 years before compact universal adaptors became available in about 1990.

Travel with a disability II

In 1987, I went to America for the wedding of Swany America's sales representative Bruce and his wife Naomi, carrying just an attaché case. Tom, the Vice President of Swany America, introducing me, said 'Next time President Miyoshi comes, he will carry all his belongings in his pockets,' to roars of laughter from the assembled guests.

I would always take my case with me when leaving my hotel room, and go straight to my first meeting after breakfast, without returning to my room. This is because the number of visits in that day depended on whether I could get my first appointment early in the morning. As my father used to say, 'Orders go up in proportion to time spent negotiating.' It also had the advantage of reducing the burden on my feet.

On the street, I would ask the nearest person the way, and then start moving. When I took someone with me, it made me realise just how much unnecessary walking people without a disability do. Before a meeting, I would have lunch somewhere nearby to avoid unexpected delays.

In a Chinese restaurant, I would have fried rice with fish and vegetables, at McDonald's I would have Filet-O-Fish and orange juice. In North America, I found Tropicana grapefruit juice particularly good. I liked the ice cream, too. If my customer was a long way away, I bought lunch from McDonald's and ate it in the taxi.

When travelling by plane I follow my parents' example and go economy class. This is better for the environment as well as easier on the wallet. Shūzaburō Kagiyama, founder of the Yellow Hat auto parts and accessories chain, who launched the 'Keep Japan Beautiful' campaign and made a name for himself promoting the benefits of toilet cleaning, is another advocate of economy class travel.

He says he once heard from an executive of Japan Air Lines that economy class is actually a goldmine, because in first class if you offer a passenger a bottle of wine costing tens of thousands of yen, you're likely to be told 'Give me some good caviar to go with it,' and if you have to open a tin of caviar costing tens of thousands of yen it's not profitable.

In 2007 I attended the 92nd World Esperanto Congress, held in Yokohama. I left a note in my hotel room saying, 'I'll be staying for one week. No need to change the sheets.' This is also Kagiyama's advice. In the evening, I returned to find the house cleaner kneeling on the floor, bowing her head deeply and saying 'Thank you for your consideration about the sheets. I'm really grateful.' 'Please get up off the floor,' I said, feeling moved to tears myself by this demonstration of gratitude.

Following Kagiyama's teaching, whenever I use the toilet in a hotel or on a plane, I always give it a wipe with a tissue before leaving and remove any hairs or specks of dust. In motorway service areas and railway stations, too, I follow the rule of 'thinking of the next process as the customer'. I don't use the razors, creams, or hair gels provided in hotels. I use the soap only if I've run out of my own.

Swany's rules for travel expenses are the same whether you're an employee or the President: ¥1,500 for meals, actual cost of travel tickets and ¥20 per kilometre for car travel.

Giving up sleeping tablets

The majority of people suffer from jet lag, while a minority seem not to be troubled by it at all. Unfortunately, I belong to the first group. Those who don't suffer seem able to sleep soundly while on the plane and to have no trouble sleeping the night after their arrival. I really envy them.

Although I don't drink alcohol, one night in Frankfurt, unable to sleep, I decided about daybreak to have a large whisky, and I fell into a drunken sleep. Come morning, my drunkenness still hadn't worn off, and I was sick by the side of the road getting a taxi. I had no choice but to keep my appointment with the buyer in this state, embarrassing though it was. I was also once told by a customer in New York, 'You smell of drink, you know.' All this was the doing of the dreaded jet lag.

The night after arriving in Europe or America, I would wake up at hourly intervals during the night, and this played havoc with my condition. This would continue for several days, and just as I was starting to get used to being in a new time zone it was time for me to fly home. Back in Japan, I would suffer again from sleepless nights. At one point, I started to rely on sleeping tablets when travelling between continents. After reaching the age of 60 it got worse, and before long I was getting prescriptions from two doctors and taking double the dose, I was in such a bad way.

In February 2019, I found myself unable to sleep even after taking three times the normal dose. This frightened me and I resolved to give up the sleeping tablets right then. I endured five endless nights without getting a wink of sleep, by the end of which in the morning my jaw was shaking, and my teeth chattered continually for the one or two hours till morning. After this I started to get a little shallow sleep, and eventually I was able to get half a night's sleep, although I still suffered from constipation.

In a few weeks, I started dozing as before, and I experienced a few more sleepless nights, after which I started dozing off again for a few more weeks. This went on for about six months before I was finally free of my dependence on sleeping tablets.

During this time, if I woke up after one or two hours' sleep, I would spend half an hour doing Nishi-shiki gymnastics before going back to bed. If I hadn't known these exercises, I think I would have been in a much worse state.

Keeping records

I have always kept notes of things that happened to me, first in reports on my business trips for the executives back home, and second as entries in my diary. But, when I stepped down as President in 2018, and brought home what I thought were all my papers, I found that my business trip reports were all missing. These were full of details of who I had met and when, what we talked about, and my own thoughts on the meeting. This book is therefore based solely on my diaries.

My diaries now span a half-century. I keep a record of postcards I've sent and replies I've received, one line for my card, with the person's name on the left and the main points of my card on the right. I make a note of the reply I received on the next line.

I draw diagrams of seating plans at meetings and write a summary of the conversation. This helps me to remember faces. I also record words that stayed in my memory, and dates.

I have made use of my business trip reports and notebook entries in writing articles for the media. I have authored many articles for newspapers and magazines, and nearly all of them are based on my notebooks.

Looking back, I see in 1966, when I was on a train from New York to Gloversville, my train collided with a dump truck. I was thrown out into the aisle, but fortunately I wasn't injured. It's there in my notebook.

Then there was the time in 1970, when I was in the German department store Karstadt. I was on the escalator facing backwards, taking a photo of the store, and reaching the next floor before I expected to, I fell flat, much to the amusement of those around me.

In 1980, I met the golfer Jack Nicklaus in Florida, and in 2011 I met Norihiro Akahoshi of the Hanshin Tigers baseball team during filming for the NHK TV business programme *Jar of Luzon*.

In a notebook from 2012, there is a record of the opening of Swany Cambodia in Phnom Penh. There are the names of the guests and the seating plan.

In 2020, while re-reading my notebooks, I was reminded of having let down the campaigner Michiko Yamamoto, when I was the Vice President of Kagawa Animal Welfare long ago. I sent her a picture postcard to apologise and received a long report on her recent activities in reply.

I'm glad to have been able to make up with her while I'm still in this world.

Improving communication skills

One of the books I have learned from is *Jacked Up*, about Jack Welch, who was the Chairman of General Electric. Welch is a legendary business leader who reigned over GE for 20 years in the 1980s and 1990s, during which time GE increased its market capitalisation by 40 times. According to Welch, he set 'choosing the right project and focussing on it' and 'improving communication skills' as his core tasks in management.

As for the former, I agree with a lot of what he says as it relates to the glove business.

Regarding the latter, he advocates pruning text four or five times, making sure you've removed any difficult words and specialist jargon, and asking yourself again if you can't say what you want to say in fewer words. This, after all, is the man who shortened 'General Electric' to 'GE'.

His emphasis on conciseness and clarity strikes me as applying to me particularly.

At one time, I was asked to serve as Chairman of the Higashikagawa Tourism Association. Every year we held a 'World Doll Festival'. The panels explaining the countries whose dolls were exhibited ran to about five or six lines of close print, and people were hardly bothering to read them. From the following year, we reduced the explanations to a maximum two lines of large characters one centimetre tall. As an example, the explanation of Belize became:

> An English-speaking country in the northeast of Central America. A little larger than Shikoku, population 310,000, average annual income ¥800,000. *Jewel of the Caribbean* surrounded by coral reefs. Famous as a holiday resort, with 450 outlying islands.

The visitors welcomed the change, saying that they got a better idea of the countries exhibiting.

His ideas on giving speeches ('You can persuade an audience in ten minutes, no matter how difficult the subject') were of use to me when I had the once-in-a-lifetime opportunity of addressing the Polish parliament, which I shall return to later in this book.

Some years ago, at the Chūgoku and Shikoku Esperanto Congress in Kotohira, the speaker before me overran by 15 minutes, and I had a difficult time cutting my own carefully crafted speech down from one hour to forty-five minutes, several times getting stuck. It was with relief that I managed to finish on time, which is another of Welch's rules.

Graph paper – the fount of wisdom

For many years, I have carried around with me a 30-hole A4 binder containing graph paper and used it to make notes and drawings. Graph paper played a large part in the development of the bag and wheelchair that marked the beginning of Swany's move away from dependence on gloves. My graph paper played a role also in the design of our overseas factories.

In 2008, I spent a week working on the design of the new Swany Cambodia factory, hoping to build on our experiences in Japan, Korea, and China. Our task was to match basic considerations of framework, plumbing and design with our objectives of ample light, insulation and airproofing, and a generally bright and work-facilitating environment.

Swany Cambodia's premises consist of a factory of 108 × 40 m, an office of 24 × 10 m, a single-storey canteen of 24 × 15 m, and a two-storey dormitory of 16 × 8 m (64 m^2 × 4). What surprised me was that a height of at least six metres was needed for the single-storey factory, enough for two storeys. This was so that the hot air could rise to the top, so that the work area below stayed cool.

Based on these considerations and objectives, I worked on the warehouse first and then moved on to the cutting and sewing areas, but because the power costs were several times what they were in other overseas locations, air conditioning turned out to be a major problem. After several years of trial and error on site, we settled on a system with underground water flowing through a heat exchanger and 12 large fans for air circulation. Another problem was mould caused by the high humidity. All this was worked out on graph paper.

We have had some failures in factory construction. When the Swany Asia factory in Korea was completed, we found that there was a difference in floor level of 5 cm at the entrance to the office, which caused us much trouble. In Cambodia, between the factory and the office I was surprised to see a floor-level difference of 15 cm. We managed somehow to make it flat, but it made me keenly aware of the importance of on-site supervision.

My work was branching out into factory design, bags, and wheelchairs, but graph paper was the source of all wisdom. I would often make drawings before going to bed at night, and when I did this, I frequently got ideas in dreams in the early hours before waking.

7. Learning from all around me

Learning from air travel

This is an old story. The first passenger plane to fly faster than the speed of sound was a Douglas DC-8. Its cruising speed was 870 kph, but in 1961, three years before I first flew, a DC-8 reached a speed slightly higher than Mach 1 (1225 kph).

This plane had rows of three seats either side of a central aisle, and the seats at the back were set aside for the crew to take rests. When the 'fasten seat belts' light went out, I would get up and move to the empty seats at the back. I had a 70% or 80% chance of finding three seats together. I would put away the armrests and lie face up, using the middle seat belt to hold my body in place. It was like a sleeper on a train, slightly cramped, but in this way I could cross continents lying down.

When travelling from Tokyo Haneda to New York I used JAL flight 005, coming back on flight 006. In the 1970s and 1980s, when I was flying frequently, a cabin crew member who I knew once gave me a gift which was for the first-class passengers, telling me to keep it a secret. The four or five cabin crew flew from Haneda to Anchorage in Alaska, where they stayed overnight, flew from there to New York the next day, and after an overnight stay in New York flew back to Anchorage, and after another overnight stay in Anchorage flew back to Japan on the fourth day.

In the late 1960s, I was on a Boeing 707 from Frankfurt to New York. After about three hours, the plane came down to just above the surface of the sea. The passenger next to me said, 'Don't worry! Three of our four engines are working!' which just made me more worried. The plane made an emergency landing in Iceland and was repaired in six hours.

In the restaurant at Kuala Lumpur Airport in Malaysia, I once found myself at the same table for lunch as my pilot and family. 'I'll invite you to the flight deck later,' he said, and he did just that soon after take-off. We landed at Kota Kinabalu in Borneo, and I was able to enjoy the spectacular scenery all the way to Manila.

In the 1970s, when I flew from Haneda to Manila with the son of the CEO of American glove company Gates on Arabian Airlines, we were caught up in a typhoon and the plane started to shake. Things started to fly around in the cabin and crash all around us, and women began to scream for help.

The passenger next to me started to recite Buddhist sutras. For the one hour it took before things calmed down, I repeated Oomoto prayers.

'Don't let me die yet!' I prayed. 'Let me live for the sake of my daughters Ayako, Masako and Yasuko!'

I didn't think about my wife Yoshiko or about the company. This was perhaps partly because my daughters were still small at the time, but it seems that at times like this one's first thoughts are of one's children. When we landed safely at Manila Airport spontaneous applause broke out from the passengers.

When I flew from Montreal in Canada to Helsinki in Finland once in the late 1980s, I noticed after boarding the Finnair night flight that there was a partition screen closing off everything beyond the fifth seat, and there were only 30 passengers on board. The backs of the seats had been lowered, and it was being used as a mixed freight/passenger plane.

I have flown 100 times between Japan and America, 50 times between Japan and Europe, 150 times between Japan and Korea, and 300 times between Japan and China, the equivalent of circling the globe 150 times.

I couldn't possibly face climate activist Greta Thunberg with my record of air travel with its high energy consumption – I would be too ashamed.

Learning from hotels

This is an embarrassing story from the 1970s.

I was in a room on the fifth floor of a hotel in Düsseldorf, drinking a cola. Without thinking, I opened a window and rested the bottle on the window frame. The next moment, the bottle fell off, and I cried out, but it was too late. The bottle hit the back of a Mercedes with people standing around. Alarmed, I went and hid under the bedclothes, pretending to be asleep.

A man from the hotel came to my room. 'Did you just throw a bottle out of the window?' I should have apologised straight away, but instead I fibbed, 'I don't know anything, I've been asleep.'

The men left the room, but presently they came back and said, 'You're the only one it could have been.' The matter was settled by my paying about ¥50,000 in compensation. The words of the saying 'Telling fibs is the first step on the road to being a thief' came to me, and I did some serious soul-searching.

In 1971, I was in the Royal Hotel in Seoul's Myeongdong district and was shocked to see smoke billowing from the 22-storey Taeyongak Hotel nearby, and people falling from the windows. Helicopters circled above with rope ladders lowered to rescue the people in the hotel, but one couple fell back to the roof while being carried to the next building.

I was shaking with terror. This fire resulted in 163 people losing their lives and 63 injuries. Many helicopters were mobilised, but most of them could do no more than circle round the hotel. They were unable to land because of an antenna installed on the roof. While the hotel was still burning, I left Seoul and took the train to Taegu, 200 or more kilometres to the south. Arriving at my hotel, I asked for a room on the ground or first floor but was told that the bottom five floors were all full. Everyone had had the same idea, wanting to avoid the higher floors.

Once in the 1980s, I was sleeping in my room in the Statler Hilton in Detroit, when the telephone rang in the middle of the night. At the other end, someone was talking excitedly, but I couldn't make out what they were saying. Then I heard the sound of people running in the corridor outside. 'Fire!' I thought and put my jacket on and ran down the stairs for my life. Down in the lobby, hundreds of people were standing around.

The hotel guests started talking to each other. Someone asked me where I had come from, and I explained that I had come from Shikoku Island in Japan. As the sky outside was starting to grow light, people came round with drinks and sandwiches. After a bomb search squad had checked all the rooms, we were finally free to go back about midday. There had been a telephone bomb scare.

But these experiences were all instructive. In hotel fires, many people went out without their room keys, and died in the corridor, unable to return to their rooms. By crawling on the floor and breathing as low as possible it is possible to survive for tens of minutes, and if one can return to one's room, there is a chance of being rescued by the fire brigade or otherwise escaping somehow. I learned that you should never forget to take your key.

Learning from Mr Cohen

In 1960, when we were selling through Strong, the export brokers in Kobe, we had a meeting with Mr Grisman Jr of the major Canadian company Grisman, Tokyo Branch Manager Cohen, and the section manager of Strong, in a building next door to the Imperial Hotel in Tokyo. It was in November, the time of year when it becomes clear how sales are doing.

While we were having lunch at the Imperial Hotel, I dropped my steak on the floor. I felt really embarrassed, and I got up and went to the toilet, where I stayed for about five minutes, hiding. When I returned to the table, I saw there was a brand-new steak waiting for me.

Mr Cohen saved the mood, praising me to the skies and calling me a 'glove wizard'.

He was in control of the whole meeting. 'So Jelmin costs ¥740 a metre, does it? How much do you need for one dozen pairs?' 'You need 0.43 metres.' 'Fuji Sangyo said 0.41,' he came back. Adding on lining, labour and packaging himself, he asked, 'How much margin do you need?' '30%,' I replied. 'They'll never sell at that price! We can only go up to 25%.' All this happened so fast I barely had time to look at my abacus or slide rule. After receiving the order, we got a lower price for the materials, and we were able to secure a margin of 30% (43% of the cost price).

Mr Cohen, who was Jewish, came to Japan as one of General Douglas MacArthur's six interpreters just after the war. He bought a plot of land about 330 m² in area in the centre of Tokyo for ¥1 million, or two months' salary, and built a new house there where he lived with his Japanese wife. At a time when the starting salary for a male university graduate was about ¥10,000 a month, he was earning half a million. When he left his post, he sold their house, which had gone up in price to about ¥300 million, and moved to a luxurious mansion with a swimming pool in Guadalajara, Mexico.

He was a tough negotiator when it came to business, but he was kind to me and considerate about my disability, and I am indebted to him for his guidance. He patiently taught me about calculation, and offered me advice on my English study, stressing the importance of repeated practice speaking out loud. He was actually my first English teacher.

It was also from Mr Cohen that I learned how to record one item per line. Face material 2 m × ¥500 = ¥1,000, lining material 2 m × ¥300 = ¥600, labour ¥800 + packaging ¥100 = cost price ¥2500. At 30% margin on the selling price + 5% for Strong, the index was 430% (at ¥360 to the dollar), giving a price per dozen of $10.70. I could record 40 to 50 items on each page in this way.

More than ten years later, I visited the United States with my wife for the first time for the Oomoto art exhibition in New York. Since it was on the way, we flew via Mexico and paid a visit to Mr and Ms Cohen. We stayed two nights with the Cohens at their huge mansion with its own guest house and accommodation for gardener and house cleaner.

After being shown around the town in Mr Cohen's Mercedes, we were having dinner. I casually said something about how nice it would be if the Israelis and Arabs could make peace. Mr Cohen's face suddenly became flushed with anger, and he said something like 'Those savages can go to the Devil for all I care.' We were flabbergasted. Even Ms Cohen couldn't do anything to calm him down. It was a shame that the mood was spoiled in this way during our visit.

He seemed to be saying that for Jewish people, 'making peace with the Arabs' was simply out of the question. And he was such a good, kind man. The deep historical, cultural, and religious roots of this entrenched enmity are hard for us Japanese to understand. We left, mindful of the difficulty of achieving world peace.

Learning from accidents

Another story.

On the evening of 13 July 1977, I was invited to dinner by the CEO of NY Glove and his wife, across from Manhattan Island. Just after eight o'clock, the glittering skyscrapers of Manhattan suddenly went dark.

There had been a major power failure. The server came, and my hosts paid the bill by the light of the candle on our table.

The traffic lights were out, and the road back to the hotel was one long traffic jam. I eventually got back to the hotel, where of course the lifts were out of action, so I had to climb the stairs to the 10th floor. The air conditioning was off, and there wasn't even any water coming out of the taps. I tried washing my face in cola, which made me feel sticky, so I washed it again with beer, which felt better. Opening the window just made the continuous wail of emergency sirens louder, and I didn't get a wink of sleep all night.

I heard that at Kennedy, La Guardia and Newark Airports, the headlights of all the cars of the airport staff were used to light up the runways so that planes could land. There was widespread theft, looting and violence, and scenes of the darkened city were broadcast to the outside world by live TV.

Thousands of people were trapped in lifts. Most were taken to the nearest floor by moving the lift carriages up or down manually, but in some places, rescuers had to break holes in the walls to free those trapped inside. In the Empire State Building there were 73 lifts, but because the blackout occurred at eight in the evening most people had already gone home, and fewer people were trapped than might have been.

Years later I watched an in-flight movie about the blackout, which mentioned that nine months later an unusually large number of babies were born.

Once, I had taken a folding bicycle from Japan to New York. I was eating at a restaurant, when the server alerted me to the fact that my bicycle's chain had been cut. I went to the scene as fast as I could to find just the chain lying on the ground. The bicycle had gone, only minutes after I had parked it. I was puzzled by the fact that the bicycles in New York only had a rear wheel, and now I realised why – the owners had removed the front wheels from their bicycles and taken them to their offices.

One day, I was woken in the middle of the night by a knock at the door. I warily opened the door to see a large African American woman standing there. 'I'm staying in the room next door, but I've forgotten my key. Can I use your phone?' she said, pushing the door open. 'Please go down to reception,' I said, and used all my strength to push the door shut. I had heard from a customer in New York that he had had someone using her charm to force her way into his room and felt that his life was in danger.

Ed, of the New York company Handal, was a worldly-wise character. Whenever I saw him, he would start singing *Swanee River*. When he took me out for lunch, he used to deliberately park in a no-parking space and give the police officer on duty a $10 bill. The police officer would then look after his car until he got back.

At the New York Mikado Japanese restaurant, I often saw two police officers having dinner. When the manager left at night with the day's takings, she was a target for thieves, so the police officers used to have dinner there every evening, and when the restaurant closed, they would escort her home.

I followed the advice given to me by a fellow passenger on the New York bus to keep my $20 and $50 bills wrapped up in a $1 bill, and even now I am in the habit of wrapping my ¥10,000 notes in a ¥1,000 note. My neighbour is indeed my teacher.

Learning from communication skills

Long ago, I attended a three-day course in communication skills given by Hiroshi Egawa, the founder of the Japan Language and Communication Training Centre, at a hotel in Takamatsu. It was an interesting and rewarding experience.

How not to get stage fright in front of people, how to introduce subjects, how speaking can build human relationships, all these and more were covered. Using the methods that I had learned, I introduced myself to all the participants. Then I watched a video of myself and was given advice on my habits of speech, tempo, intonation and so on.

All of us gave three-minute speeches titled 'a story of failure', 'when I praised someone' and 'what stays in my memory from this course'. Our strong points were praised, and guidance was given on how to overcome our shortcomings.

During the course, I complimented a man I met in the hotel lift on the tie he was wearing. 'Do you really like it?' the man said, delighted, and took off his tie and gave it to me. I told this story in my speech, to applause from the other participants. I remember it as if it were yesterday, although it happened 40 years ago. Ever since, I have been recommending the course to our employees.

I sent our new recruits Yoshiharu Nakanishi, Yasushi Okudai, Sakuji Imataki and Takaaki Iwaki to take the speaking course. I later received the heart-warming comment from a fellow participant, 'Seeing how proactive they were in speaking, I could see how good your company is at training its staff.'

Another old story – a number of leading members of the local women's association visited our house. They proposed that my wife, who was in her forties at the time, become president of the association, but she declined, saying that she didn't have the qualities and lacked confidence speaking in public.

I suggested to my wife that she take the speaking course. After I had made the suggestion several times, she finally agreed, but afterwards she said she still felt unsure of herself. When I suggested giving it another try, she took the course again, and this time she seemed to have gained a little confidence.

My wife's confidence grew, and she went on to become President of Shirotori Honchō Women's Association, President of Higashikagawa Women's Association, President of the Women's Section of the Ōkawa Business Association, President of the Shirotori Branch of Oomoto, and a member of the Oomoto Council of Deputies.

Tom, the Vice President of Swany America, told me that in the United States training in public speaking was a required subject. This is no doubt why, unlike us Japanese who tend to run away from the microphone, the Americans seem reluctant to let go of it... I was reminded of this while I listened, entranced, to the election victory speeches of President Biden and Vice President Harris.

Learning from lectures

Since my youth, I have had many opportunities to speak in front of the company staff, but often I found it difficult to express myself clearly. Ordinary conversation was never a problem for me, and I couldn't understand why I was so poor at public speaking. My father constantly chided me 'Your voice is too quiet! We can't make out what you're saying!'

In about 1970, I read *Public Speaking* by Dale Carnegie. This is a self-improvement book that goes beyond speaking skills, but it's a treasure trove of advice on speaking technique: 'Talk about your own experiences,' 'Capture your audience's attention with your first word,' 'Get people to raise their hands,' and so on. Carnegie's book was a best-seller, published in 100 countries in 30 languages, and read by nine million people, and is still in print today.

After I had read it for the third time, I was invited to give a lecture. I was to speak on the subject of 'change of mindset'. I wasn't confident at all, but then I remembered the words of Carnegie's book 'If you're given the opportunity to speak, you should grab it. You won't get another chance! Even if you try to recruit an audience yourself by offering everyone 50 dollars, no one will come to hear you!'

I began my presentation with the words, 'My mind a blank, I got on my scooter and rode away.' I told the story of my unrequited love and disappearance, but I followed the book's advice about not starting with a preamble. From then on, I was able to continue without freezing. I wasn't totally satisfied with my performance, but I had changed a lot from the time when I was told off by my father for mumbling and felt embarrassed in front of an audience.

Since then, my speaking opportunities have increased, and I have given more than 200 talks in different parts of the country. Mostly these have been about my business experiences.

I did still get into trouble once, though, when I was giving a talk to the assembled pupils at the local elementary school. The first- and second-year children in the front row started throwing shoes at each other, which distracted me and made me forget what I was saying. The teacher scolded the children, but still they carried on. I realised that I needed to talk to them in children's language. These sweet little children were in fact my toughest audience.

Learning from recruitment

In the 1970s, we needed urgently to recruit new staff, but we were having little success, and there didn't seem to be a quick and easy solution.

One year, I remember we had applications from four or five students, and we held an orientation meeting at a hotel near Hiroshima Station. Only one of the applicants actually came, while from our side there were three of us, two recruitment officers and me. The interviewee must have felt awkward being faced with the company president and two others.

What was even more annoying was that the applicants we were keen on all turned us down. With recruitment, as with marriage, both sides must feel they can commit themselves, otherwise it won't work. We had to attract them somehow.

There was only one way. We had to make ourselves attractive. We had to show the students straight away that the President was a trustworthy character with a good reputation in the local community. So, in our information pack we included an appraisal of Swany by Nobuo Kanayama, a well-known pioneering teacher of simultaneous interpreting, as well as a commentary by the popular author Yūsuke Fukada. We also included a few articles from the press for them to read.

In 1979, Swany and the supermarket chain Sunny Mart, based in Kōchi in southern Shikoku, shared the *Shikoku Shimbun* newspaper award for best advertisement, with a recruiting advertisement featuring a photograph of Diane, my English teacher from Florida. These efforts bore fruit and for a while we made it into the 'ten most popular companies' among students in Kagawa.

But it didn't all go smoothly. One year, a student from Tokushima University who we had shortlisted told us, 'I'm not sure I'd want to work in a company that uses leather.' Noticing that he was wearing leather shoes, I unthinkingly answered, 'You don't mind animals dying for your shoes, though, do you?'

About this time, I asked the staff if they could recommend potential recruits, and one employee came back with the harsh reply, 'The boss is extreme in his likes and dislikes and lacks tolerance. He's always finding fault with people. Improve that image and then people will come.' I was quite distressed for days after this, the words 'likes and dislikes', 'tolerance' and 'image' rising unbidden to my mind. I had given them a big stick to beat me with!

As if to put paid to all hope, Senior Executive Director Mitsunaka put it bluntly at one meeting: 'I'm afraid you just won't get the kind of staff you want in a seasonal industry like glove-making.' I found it impossible to argue with him.

Learning from advice

To write this book, I reread a half-century's worth of diaries. They made for hard reading and gave rise to much soul-searching. I found these points raised by Junji Yagi, who joined the company in 1976:

1. Criticisms should be made at the time and in private.
2. The wages are those of a small to medium company.
3. People's opinions aren't listened to.
4. Only Junior Executive Director Iwazawa has any influence over the President.
5. People are unhappy about senior appointments.
6. People are concerned at the retirement of senior executives.
7. The Chairman (my father) should be treated with more respect.

Pay levels, not paying attention to the staff's opinions, no one to restrain me, unconvincing appointments, worrying numbers of people leaving, treatment of my father... on each and every point there was no room for excuses. I was made painfully aware of what a poor boss I was.

I am reminded of Hidemaru Deguchi's words, 'If you can change yourself even just a little, your life can take a 180-degree turn.'

Executive Director Iwazawa left the company, but for 10 years he had doubts about the leadership of the business. 'Unless you understand your own company, no amount of study of management theory will give you any results. Improvements could have been made without wasteful spending if we had just discussed things within the company,' he said.

When making medium-term business plans, I thought there was value in repeating the plan-do-check-act cycle and using human resource development consultants. But being told that things could have improved if there had just been more discussion, I couldn't help feeling regret.

I had been taught to praise people in writing and admonish them orally, but I had been doing the opposite, and committing blunders. Once, I sent an email to Section Manager Takaaki Iwaki, who made a video about the Swany Bag, saying 'If you had written a script first, you could have got it down to within two minutes,' before giving him a chance to explain that the camera operator had instructed him to speak freely without a script. I immediately regretted it, but it was already too late.

Learning from language study

I encourage the staff to study English conversation because I had such a hard time with it myself.

Since the 1970s, Swany has hired many English instructors, and about a hundred staff have learned with them. The results haven't quite come up to our highest expectations, through no fault of the teachers, although the staff have at least become more familiar with English...

In 1977, Korean staff members Go Yeong-bae and Ju Byeong-su went to learn Japanese and Tsukasa Itano and a few dozen others went to learn English at a language school in Takamatsu. Their fees for individual tuition were ¥4,000 for a 40-minute lesson, and although the results were outstanding, their tuition cost a million yen per pupil for a month.

I started learning Korean in 1975, three years after our expansion into Korea. I took lessons from a Berlitz teacher for seven hours every day for four months. I found it so similar to Japanese in its grammar that I thought the Japanese language must have come from Korean. It is by far the easiest language for Japanese people to learn.

Once, when I arrived at Busan Airport, the immigration officer asked me where I had learned Korean. 'Berlitz hakkyoro paeusumnida' (I learned at the Berlitz school), I replied, and he complimented my pronunciation and gave me a firm welcome handshake.

In 2017, Itano, my successor as President, initiated daily 25-minute English conversation lessons for 13 staff with the online school Bizmates. Students can learn wherever they are, provided they have access to a computer. Bizmates is a specialist English conversation school for businesspeople with 400 instructors. All of them are experienced English teachers from the Philippines, and the monthly tuition fee is a reasonable ¥12,000 per student.

The instructors are friendly and skilled at teaching, and from what I have seen it seems to me that a year of study would be enough to give my proficiency a significant boost.

Learning from the toilet

In the restroom at Paris Glove in Montreal, Canada, I found the urinals too high for comfort. I was just too short. It bothered me so much that I mentioned it to the divisional manager, who was about the same height as me, and he laughed and said, 'Well, use the sit-down toilet!'

I remember as a young man being at the house of an Oomoto member at the foot of Konpira Shrine, where they had a sign that read, in classical Japanese verse form, 'With calmness of mind / use your hand to guide it straight / dew of the mushroom.'

When I visited the men's toilet in the old Hongqiao Airport in Shanghai in 1988, I was pleased to find that, although I couldn't speak Chinese, I could clearly understand the request to 'move forward one step' – an advantage of our shared writing system!

In the restroom at Avon in New York, they had this sign: 'Don't believe yours is so long.'

In 2005 I travelled to Vilnius in Lithuania to attend the World Esperanto Congress. My companions and I travelled by minibus from Warsaw in neighbouring Poland. The country of Lithuania is well known to the Japanese for the actions of Chiune Sugihara, the deputy consul at the Japanese Consulate in Kaunas, in issuing visas to 6,000 Jewish refugees fleeing Europe at the beginning of World War II, for which he is remembered as one of the 'Righteous Among the Nations'. Having just crossed the border into Lithuania, we stopped at a filling station, and went to the toilet. It was so spotlessly clean that we couldn't bring ourselves to use it. We later stopped again and relieved ourselves in the woods.

I have experienced many toilets, in Korea, in China, in Ethiopia and elsewhere. In 1960s Japan, while out visiting subcontractors, I got heartily sick of the intense smell from the old-fashioned latrines.

At Toa Leather, where my father was a director, the night soil was sold by auction. In those days, night soil was such a valuable commodity that the staff used to suppress the urge to go to the toilet and rush home at the end of the day so that it would not be wasted.

When we were running factories in Tokushima, I went to the toilet at Tokushima Swany, and found that there was no toilet paper. Unable to find anything else, I tore off the bottom half of my undershirt and used that. Back home, I was getting into the bath, and Yoshiko said, 'What on earth happened to your vest?' I had completely forgotten about the incident in the toilet.

At Swany China, the pigs were waiting hungrily below the toilet seat. I can't be the only one to feel sorry for those Chinese pigs who had only such miserable fare to look forward to.

At the 2007 World Esperanto Congress in Yokohama, I listened to a talk given by a participant from Russia, who commented on the clean and spacious Japanese toilets for the disabled: 'If you put a bed in there, it would be nicer than my own bedroom back home.'

Learning from Yoshiko

Ever since we got married, my wife Yoshiko and I bathed together. When my youngest daughter Yasuko was at elementary school, after dinner, she said, 'Papa, tonight I'll give you a bath. You can't have a bath on your own, can you?' As I approach old age, Yoshiko still lets me get in the bath with her, while laughingly complaining that it's too cramped.

Once, after practising my Nishi-shiki gymnastics, I was feeling rather tired, and without thinking, I rested my elbows on the dinner table. 'What are you doing?' Yoshiko said. 'I'm sorry, I'm a bit tired...' I said, but she came back, 'It's no use apologising to me!'

When I was young, we had a visitor at night. I showed them out, and our visitor closed the gate, so I went to switch off the outside light. Yoshiko scolded me, 'You mustn't switch the light off yet. You must leave it on until our guest has disappeared from sight. Just because they've left the house it doesn't mean you can forget about them.'

Whenever we have a guest, Yoshiko starts tidying and cleaning all around the house. If I say, 'Surely that's enough now,' she says, 'No, it isn't enough!' and carries on tidying. That's enough now,' I say, but she doesn't listen. If you can't beat them, join them, I decide, and I start picking up pieces of dust. At home, the pocket of my Swany Bag is our wastebasket.

Every morning, after shaving and combing my hair, she tells me my hair is split at the back and smooths it for me, wetting the comb so that it doesn't split. 'If you button your shirt right up to the top it looks awful!' 'Zip your trousers up all the way!' she constantly reminds me. 'And when the phone rings, answer it straight away!'

About two years ago, I had a major scare. 'You're always talking about equality of the sexes, why not take your turn cooking the dinner?' After much thought, I found a way to fend off this threat by giving her neck and shoulders a good 15-minute massage before going to sleep every night.

The subject of personal appearance reminds me of the novel serialised in the *Nikkei* newspaper in 2019, *Michikusa-sensei* by Shizuka Ijūin, a story about the early 20th-century Japanese author Natsume Sōseki. In the novel, Sōseki learns from his elder brother that 'Most people measure others' calibre by their appearance.' 'Appearance? Calibre?' asks Sōseki. 'Exactly. Their calibre as a person. They judge it by looking at people's grooming and appearance.'

It was Hiroko Ikeda of the 'Human Science Research Institute' who taught me thirty years ago to keep a hand mirror on my desk. Seeing my reflection in the mirror, which I have fixed to my desktop organiser, enables me to check my appearance, if not the back of my head. I have also learned to keep my things in one place so that I don't spend time looking for them...

Between us, I think my wife with her penetrating sensibility and I with my thick skin make quite a well-balanced pair.

Learning from typing

In 1964 I started going on overseas business trips accompanied by interpreters. I would convey the orders back by telephone, and our long-serving colleague Hatsuo Matsumura typed the order acknowledgement, which he would then post to the customer by way of confirmation.

Details of size, materials and the like were typed on the trusty Olivetti typewriter. I found typing quite easy, and after about a week practising for half an hour every day, I became familiar enough with the layout of the keys to type using all my fingers without looking at the keyboard.

When I switched to using a word processor, the shop assistant persuaded me to go for the 'thumb-shift' Japanese keyboard, which used one key for two characters. I found it considerably harder than the Latin keyboard, but I managed to learn the character layout in about a month. I carried my Fujitsu 'OASYS Pocket' around with me wherever I went. After a few years, I found I could type on it even on the bus when all around me was dark. I no longer wrote reports on business meetings by hand but typed them on my word processor instead.

With the arrival of Microsoft, the thumb-shift keyboard became an extinct species, and, at the age of more than sixty, I had to set about learning the JIS kana keyboard layout, which I found a good 20% slower.

At Swany headquarters, where about a hundred staff now operate PCs, we started to encourage touch-typing in 2017, offering a prize of ¥10,000 for reaching grade A and another ¥10,000 for reaching the highest grade. We had 11 staff who were already proficient touch-typists, and a further 28 have now won prizes, meaning that the proportion of touch-typists has increased from 10% to 40%.

According to management consultant and author Kenichi Ohmae, in Korea and China junior high school students were encouraged to master touch-typing by giving them a whack on the shoulder when they tried to peek. I worry about the future of Japan, 20 years late in digitisation and way behind in typing speed...

Learning from reading

When I was at senior high school, by the third lesson of the day I would start eating my lunch, hiding behind the textbook. My grades were average or below, and I never really studied seriously.

Mr Page, the Director of Language House in Takamatsu, always used to say, 'If your Japanese is sound, and you're good at karaoke, you'll be good at speaking English.' I can speak some English, but I can't write it, and it looks likely that I'll never even be able to write so much as a postcard in Japanese without needing a dictionary.

In his book *Letters of a Businessman to His Son*, Kingsley Ward wrote, 'However much reading you do, if you read nothing but novels, you're wasting your time. There's so much to learn from reading non-fiction.'

Carl Hilty advised his readers to 'adopt regular reading habits from an early age, and not to read worthless books'.

Of course, I recognise that this is rather an extreme view, and I'm sure there are many worthwhile novels to be read, but I endeavour to read as much non-fiction as I can. And yet, if you asked me what I've learned from my reading, I'd find it hard to tell you. The value of experience is well expressed by my life's guide, Hidemaru Deguchi: 'Books are fine, but gaining experiences is the most important thing you can do.'

In 2014, I joined the Sapie Library, an online library that provides an audio book service for the visually impaired. There are about 500,000 audio books available, which have been recorded by 220 groups across the country. The ability to lie back and listen to books being read with one's eyes closed is invaluable, and the recordings are most captivating. To take an example, Donald Keene, the American-born scholar of Japanese literature, wrote about 45 books in Japanese, of which 26 are available as audio books.

I came to know about this library after I began to find reading for long periods difficult following a cataract operation, and an old friend from high school Rikuo Satō told me about it. I registered by going to the Kagawa Prefectural Library in Takamatsu and filling in a form describing the extent of my impairment. Once registered, I was provided with a dedicated software application costing about ¥20,000 to download to my PC, giving me access to all their wonderful readings.

Funnily, however, I find that I don't remember books as well afterwards when they're read for me as I do when I read them myself, so I buy books that have interested me and read them again. On Internet mail order sites, you can find books for as little as ¥1, and you can have them delivered to your door the next day for only about ¥250 delivery charge. I now also get books from the likes of Amazon and Rakuten.

Learning from prayer

For the last half-century, I have attended morning prayers at 6.30 every morning at the Shirotori Branch of Oomoto, and on the first day of every month prayed also at Shirotori Shrine, a custom started by my father. After prayers, I went to work and turned on the air conditioning ready for a seven o'clock start.

I have also had experiences worshipping abroad.

One Sunday towards the end of the year, I walked north from the centre of Helsinki for 15 minutes when the temperature was -30°C, my knees shaking from the cold. Arriving at the Temppeliaukio Church, carved from the rock, and following the sound of the organ, I was surprised to see a congregation of several hundred, although it was snowing heavily outside. I was the only Japanese there.

Mr Schiller, a buyer at K-Mart in Detroit, was a tough customer. The first time I met him he sent me away, saying, 'I'm the world's top buyer! I only want to see the best gloves in the world! And at the cheapest price!' After five years of tenacious efforts, however, I got to do business with him, and I once went to church with him and Ms Schiller. They were parishioners of a church called St Hugo of the Hills. This was the one and only time I attended a church service with a buyer.

Since the Oomoto exhibition *The Art of Onisaburo Deguchi and His School* was held at the Cathedral Church of St John the Divine in New York in 1975, I have attended worship at the Cathedral many times. One Sunday, after attending Holy Eucharist, I was flabbergasted to hear Dean James Parks Morton announce my presence to the congregation, asking them to welcome 'Mr Miyoshi of Oomoto'.

With Mr and Mrs Schiller at St Hugo's Church, 1978

I have also worshipped at the Church of the Incarnation, at St Michael's Cathedral in Toronto, and at the Cathedral of Saint-Jacques in Montreal. In Japan, I offer prayers at Shinto and Buddhist temples and shrines such as Heian Shrine and Kasuga Shrine. I believe that all the world's religions are connected at their root.

Japanese Shinto stresses belief in *kototama*, or the power of words. The Christian gospel, too, teaches, 'In the beginning was the word, and the word was with God, and the word was God.' My prayer is that I may give thanks for the blessings of Heaven and Earth, and contribute to the fellowship of religions, nations, and linguistic communities.

In my life so far, I have tried to learn what I can from the world around me, and to put into practice what I have learned.

PART 2.

RESPONDING TO SUPPORT NEEDS

Comments from users of the Swany Bag

'I groaned when my doctor suggested I should use a walking frame, but then I found the Swany Bag in the Keio department store. Now it goes with me everywhere.' (N, Tokyo)

'At Tokyo Station, I found there were no seats in the waiting room, and so the seat came in very handy. The bag supported me all the way down the long platform. I couldn't ask for more!' (Y, Ichihara)

'It's a hundred metres from my door to the car park, and it's like a dream being supported while carrying my luggage. It's wonderful because it gives me a feeling of security.' (H, Yokohama)

'When I meet another Swany user, even a complete stranger, we strike up a conversation about our bags, and I've already made lots of friends this way.' (I, Kanazawa)

'In Singapore, somebody asked me where I bought my bag. When I told them I bought it in Japan, they were so disappointed. I'm full of gratitude to the inventor of this great bag.' (M, Fukuoka)

In 2013 the number of Swany Bags shipped yearly rose to more than 110,000. Most of the 8,000 questionnaire postcards we receive back from customers every year express satisfaction and gratitude. But before the combined bag and walking aid appeared and gained acceptance, there were countless hurdles to be overcome.

Discovery

When I was on my third round-the-world trip in 1966, I was drawn to a luggage shop just south of the Empire State Building in New York. In the window there was a suitcase with 75 mm wheels. 'With stout wheels like those, there will be no need to lift it up!' I thought. Surprised, I doubted my eyes for a moment.

I immediately bought one for \$70 (about ¥25,000), packed my glove samples and my personal belongings in it, and walked off, leaning on my new case. When packed, the suitcase supported my entire body weight, and my heart felt a hundred times lighter. Until then, a case weighing just 15 kg had felt so heavy, I was afraid I would have to give up travelling abroad.

I bought one of these suitcases every time I visited America, and so there were about 20 of them in the company office. The staff started to use them, and they became very popular. Heavy sewing machine parts weighing more than 100 kg could be carried with ease.

When travelling abroad, I used to put my belongings in the drawers of the hotel room and took my empty suitcase with me to lean on when I went out to eat. I was regarded with suspicion when I entered department stores, and the security staff often ordered me to open my case. When they saw it was empty inside, they apologised and let me pass.

But when full of gloves, the case would weigh about 20 kg, and on stairs I would have to go up one step with my left foot while holding on to the handrail with my left hand, and pull up the case with my right hand, which meant that the burden on my left leg was double what it would be for someone with a good right leg. Even when empty, it weighed 7 kg, and getting in and out of taxis with it was a struggle.

Even so, this suitcase gave me an important hint. In wide open airport buildings, where there is nothing to hold on to for support, people with disabilities find walking difficult. Would it be possible to design a bag small enough to take on board as hand luggage, and at the same time steady enough to be leaned on like a large suitcase? If a small bag could support the body's weight, how easy it would make travelling, I thought.

Challenges in developing the walking bag

After handing over my suitcase at the airport check-in counter, I kept thinking about the idea of a briefcase with wheels and handle attached, easy to walk with anywhere! But, busy with glove-related work as the face of Swany, I let 30 years go by walking through airport buildings dreaming of a supporting wheeled bag.

With the bursting of the 'bubble economy', and with global warming starting to be felt as a reality, sales in the glove industry dropped from ¥66 billion to ¥35 billion. Developing year-round products became more urgent than ever, and in 1992 we held a series of strategy meetings, where we looked into products such as ties, hats, and work gloves. All of these were fiercely competitive markets, and it was clear that we lacked the resources to win out.

Then, my younger brother and senior executive director Asao suggested making suitcases like the ones I had bought. We made some, by copying, but the result was an amateurish failure. We then decided to attempt making the compact body-supporting bag that I had been dreaming about all those years.

In 1995 we started work on the prototype support bag. Our task was to make a product with a handle that can support the body without buckling, and with wheels that rotate freely.

We had the idea of a bag divided by a partition in the centre, with the handle attached to this dividing wall. Because the inside of the bag was split into two separate compartments, this could only hold relatively thin items, and we had difficulty in selling it. But the feedback from those who did buy it was 'This is the kind of bag I've been looking for.'

I continued the quest for a bag that could hold larger items and that still supported the body. The problem was that unless the handle was in the middle it wouldn't provide the necessary support but having the handle in the middle meant the bag couldn't hold large items. My colleague Yoshio Takahara, armed with legendary dexterity and a full set of machine tools, proceeded with development, trying an extendable ladder-like arrangement, but this was rejected as being too unstable.

Having to rely on Chinese parts for reasons of cost, I visited Shanghai in 1996 for discussions with luggage parts manufacturers, but without success. One night, exhausted, I went to my hotel room to sleep, and woke in the middle of a dream in which I had the idea of bending the tubular sections of the telescopic handle. I jumped out of bed and got out my graph paper and started drawing. By giving the handle at the side a curve with a radius of five metres, we could bring the handle grip in line with the middle of the bag when extended. I was sure this would solve the problem of stability.

'You've done it!' I cried out.

But as yet this was a success only on paper. When we asked five of the major Japanese aluminium manufacturers if they could make curved tubes in three thicknesses (thick, medium, and thin), they all answered that it was impossible. We then approached ten handle manufacturers in Taiwan, but their reply was the same. One company alone said that they could cut the tubes to the required length and give them a curve with a radius of five metres using a hydraulic device. After dozens of trials, the Swany Bag, the 'walking handrail' that I had been dreaming of for 30 years, was finally born.

The invention of a wheeled bag pushed at the side while supporting the body instead of being pulled behind brought about a transformation in the world of luggage.

Edison said, 'Invention is 1% inspiration and 99% perspiration,' and this was the case with my bag – the 1% of inspiration made all the effort worthwhile.

Long road to acceptance

The achievement of the long-sought after body-supporting 'walking bag' was a cause for jubilation, but we were still faced with the task of marketing. Contrary to my expectations, sales didn't grow at all for three years.

Wanting to popularise this bag by hook or by crook, I took it round to luggage shops all over the country myself. Many of the shop staff responded by denying that a body-supporting bag could be a reality, and others even refused to believe that there could be any demand for such a thing. About 10% of the shop managers I visited did take a few, however, saying 'My grandmother might like it' or some such, and the number of shops taking them gradually increased. Presently, we started to get feedback that there were people who said they liked the bag, and we knew that there was a demand after all.

But then a powerful 'enemy within' emerged. Six division heads at the company, none of them disabled, couldn't understand the needs of people with disabilities. At every monthly meeting, these six pressed for withdrawal from the bag market. I could understand their anxiousness to avoid bankruptcy, and I felt isolated and embattled. Seeing me pouring tens of millions of yen into this loss-making bag, they began to suggest that if I wanted to continue with this project I should do so on my own.

In September 2000, after running up cumulative losses of ¥400 million, I was faced with the choice of withdrawing or continuing. Unable to shake off my belief that one day it would find favour with the public, I decided to bite the bullet.

I told Shūji Isei, head of the bag division, that I would remove the executives that had opposed the bag from their positions and replace them with younger people. 'If you do that the company will collapse!' he protested.

In a last-ditch attempt to bring about a turnaround, I enlarged the product tag to the size of a book and included a photo of myself supporting myself with a Swany Bag, with the words, 'After travelling round the world a hundred times, suffering the after-effects of childhood polio, and thinking how travelling could be made easier, I have perfected a bag that you can lean on while walking. Etsuo Miyoshi, President of Swany glove company.'

How much this was due to the tag I don't know, but the supporting bag started to catch on, and mail-order companies used my story in their advertising. We provided 700 bags to be hired out free of charge at the Awaji Flower Expo. The newspaper *Nihon Keizai Shimbun* published a piece about the Swany Bag, and it also appeared on national TV. That autumn, we were able to celebrate reaching our sales target, the threat of dismissals passed, and the dissenting voices went quiet.

During the two years when the continued existence of the bag division was under threat, my eldest brother Hajime Tani flew down from Tokyo to take part in every monthly meeting. He was a bulwark against the six dissidents and helped me to come through this crisis. Today, the Swany Bag accounts for 25% of all our sales, and its future looks assured.

Quiet and freely rotating castors

When sales of the 'walking bag' were growing, we began to get feedback from customers that the wheels were noisy and that they sometimes lifted the bag up to avoid making too much noise. I thought hard about how we could solve this problem, and I even had difficulty sleeping at night thinking about it. This was in 2003. While I was worrying about the problem of the noisy wheels, I visited the International Home Care and Rehabilitation Exhibition at the Tokyo Big Sight Exhibition Centre, where I saw a wheelchair with a front wheel with only a single central bearing. I immediately thought of the saving in cost, noise, and weight.

Because of technical problems, however, Swany alone could not turn this into a saleable product. I visited Hammer Castor, the leading Japanese castor company, and asked their President, Haruichi Yoshida, if they could provide technical guidance on quiet and smooth castors. The technicians were assembled, and they taught me that by laying an oiled bearing on its side a castor can be made to rotate quietly and freely, but strength is reduced by about 30%, so we devised a reinforcing method, for which we obtained a patent.

To make these into saleable products, I visited Shanghai 100 times in the space of seven or eight years. After investing tens of millions of yen, we perfected a castor that would move quietly at the push of a single finger even when loaded with six two-litre bottles of water. In the eighth incarnation, a state-of-the-art 60 mm castor in which the axle and the direction-changing portion are supported by eight oil bearings made its first appearance. The wheel can also be changed easily with just a screwdriver.

'It turns like a dream, and the castors haven't broken even after ten years' use. The price is high, but it's paid for itself in the long run.' (I, Ibaraki)

'It turns freely and moves forward smoothly. Having a bad leg as I do, I'm delighted to have found this bag.' (S, Akashi)

Loved by the non-disabled

The answers to the question 'Why did you buy a Swany Bag?' in our questionnaire were: smooth running 41%, support 36%, and manoeuvrability 22%. The high proportion of users who replied 'smooth running' rather than 'support' suggests that the Swany Bag is being used by many non-disabled people. Here are some of the comments we have received.

'Thanks to its bright lining it's easy to find things inside, and all you have to do is put your hand on it and it moves with you. It's easier than walking with your hands free. It's my good companion, and it carries my things for me too!' (M, Tokyo)

'I thought these bags were for the elderly, but now I've tried it I feel that the Swany is pulling me! Even with five kilos of stuff inside, I can walk as if I'm floating.' (R, Yokohama)

Bag with interchangeable wheels

JSo far, the bag had been sewn and then the frame inserted, the handle grip and tubes attached, and the wheels tacked on, but there was a multitude of processes and parts involved, and it was vulnerable to breaking and costly. I decided we should aim at a new structure which would allow any bag to be fitted over a base with wheels and handle.

This was unpopular within the company, the reason given being that people wouldn't buy a bag with the frame exposed. But the advantage was that because the bag could be easily removed, the frame and wheels, which picked up dirt from the street, could be left by the door and just the bag brought into the living area – this was the deciding factor in the patent being granted. I persevered, and today, 20 years after I first had the idea, 90% of our bags are of the removable type.

'Its advantages are capacity, lightness, ease of movement, and, above all, the fact that the bag can be detached from the frame. This is important because my daughter is obsessed with cleanliness, and she won't let me bring the frame into the room!' (S, Matsudo)

'I always remove the bag from its frame before bringing it into the room. This remarkable bag is the product of Mr Miyoshi's own life experience. I wish I'd bought one sooner!' (I, Tanba)

The disabled point of view

On reaching the age of sixty, I had a handrail fitted at the entrance of our house. Coming home, I noticed that the handrail had moved slightly to the side. My wife said she had moved it because it looked better there. I objected, from the point of view of the disabled user: 'Yes, but convenience is more important than appearance.' In the course of the exchange that followed, my wife said, 'In that case, what's the point of handing over the Swany Bag to a successor with no disability?' which stopped me in my tracks. Yes, I thought. Only someone with a disability can really understand the needs of the disabled. I decided there and then that I would hire someone with a disability.

Now working at Swany is Keiji Bandō, a designer working with computer-aided design who damaged his hip joint in an accident. He is now actively working to develop products that are just right for people with disabilities, firmly believing that they can appeal to the non-disabled, too.

'When I was about to board a plane with my Swany Bag, one of the airline staff stopped me, but when I explained that I couldn't walk without it, I was allowed through.' (Y. Machida)

'I fell into despair when I damaged my leg, but since encountering the Swany Bag, I am thankful every day. I'm now active at the local community centre and in the local choir.' (A. Kōchi)

Responding to women's needs

In 2003, the manager of a certain luggage shop in Tokyo said to me, 'Your bags are brilliant from the function point of view, but the design leaves a lot to be desired. You're not letting men do the designing, are you?' Being the culprit myself, I felt ashamed on hearing this, and I decided right then that we should employ more female staff. Just then, Misuzu Watanabe of the Administration Department expressed the wish to get involved in product planning. Her mother had a disability and she had lost a child to disease, and she wanted to put her experience to use in product planning based on the principles of universal design, which aims to make products accessible to all.

The Monogramo series, designed for the 'bright middle adult', was one of Ms Watanabe's hit designs, of which more than 50,000 were produced over 10 years. This bag, with a keynote of black and an opulent enamel lustre, had a generous capacity, making it suitable for work and for going out. Making the bag easily upwardly expandable to hold extra items was one of her innovations.

As a member of the product development team, Ms Watanabe is busy every day listening to customers' comments and relaying their wishes to the factory. She is enthusiastic about making products to support a lifestyle of going out and travelling for people who may not have been inclined to leave the house before.

'It's light and stylish, and people often compliment me on it. It brings a smile to my face.' (K. Yokohama)

'The design is high quality. People ask me, "Is it made in Italy?" It's super functional and quiet, too. The more I polish it, the more it shines. It's a real eye-opener.' (O. Kawasaki)

A handbag to lean on

In 2007, we started to receive comments from some of our female customers such as these: 'It would be nice to have a handbag I could lean on.' 'My handbag is so heavy it feels like I'm walking around with gold bars in there.' I decided to check my wife's handbag to see what it was like. Makeup, mirror, mobile phone, glasses, diary... yes, it was indeed quite a weight. This is something that we men just don't realise.

We set about creating the world's smallest wheeled bag. We started by introducing a small size of frame, which had previously come in just two sizes, large and medium. This had a floor measuring 21.5 cm × 15 cm and a height of 27 cm.

We increased the number of tubular sections from three to four. Even with a height of only 27 cm, the handle still had to come up to 90 cm. To make the approximately 20 different parts inside the handle as low as possible, we expended much ingenuity in making design adjustments at the sub-millimetre level. We ended up with a handle which, although slightly angular, could support the body's weight without the user feeling any discomfort in the palm of the hand.

'Although the handles of other brands I've tried are more streamlined, they made my hand ache two or three times more. I'm glad I went for the Swany.' (T, Shijōnawate)

'I'm of an age where I'm reluctant to use a walking stick. This bag, with its ample room, makes it a pleasure to go for walks or outings.' (K, Naha)

A bag you can sit on

Next, we started to get requests for a bag with a seat, and in 2003 we perfected the first bag with seat. However, this had a short working life because of the way the seat folded away.

The second model had a mechanical folding system, but it still wasn't one-touch. This bag was popular with our customers and continued to sell for more than five years.

Much work went into perfecting the third model, which appeared in 2015. The seat could be opened and folded away by a single touch. It has many happy users, although it does have the drawback that the seat is rather heavy.

'If I'm feeling tired, I can sit for a while and recover. I can sit down while waiting for the train, and it supports me while I'm walking. I think it's the best bag in the world.' (A, Niigata)

'My boy commutes to school with it. He can get all his books in it, and he can sit down and study while waiting on the station platform. He likes the seat!' (H, Tokyo)

Split-level bag for people with back problems

Next, to meet the needs of people who can't bend at the waist or are troubled by lower back pain, we introduced a new product with upper and lower compartments, which enabled packing and unpacking without needing to bend. This was the 'Dumano'.

'I damaged my back and can no longer bend, so I use the split-level Dumano. It's ideal for one- or two-night stays. Please make more split-level bags.' (T, Minoo)

'I can't bend because of lower back pain. Please make more kinds of Dumano. Swany Bags are absolutely indispensable for me.' (Y, Tokorozawa)

The name *Dumano* is a compound word from the Esperanto *du* (two) and *mano* (hand).

I am a user of the international language Esperanto, which is easy to learn and allows freedom to make compound words. Registering English trademarks is getting harder with every passing year, and at Swany we turn to Esperanto for our brand names. With still only about a million speakers in the world, it has hardly been exploited at all!

Birth of the four-wheel stopper

Our new products always originate from the comments of our customers. After being told by many users that the wheels ran too smoothly and needed brakes, we introduced the two-wheel and four-wheel stoppers.

When on a train, all four wheels have to be stopped. I have experienced this many times myself while travelling on the Takamatsu to Tokushima line. Even if just one wheel rotates, the bag runs away. Stopping all four swivel castors would require Nobel prize-level ingenuity. But thanks to the perseverance of Gorō Hashimoto of the servicing division, a new technology was born, which stops the bag from moving by making the four wheels perpendicular to each other.

Ideally it should be possible to do this while gripping the handle, without needing to bend down to operate a lever, but there are a number of difficulties with this due to the properties of oscillating castors. However, Swany has made possible what was thought to be impossible in the past, and we hope by using all our resources to solve this problem, too.

'The wheels on the new improved bag are bigger and less likely to get stuck in grooves, and have a stopper, too. I'm very happy with it.' (K. Tokyo)

'The stopper means I no longer have to worry. I'm a music volunteer, and things like ukuleles and music stands are likely to fall over if the wheels start rolling. But now I can rest easy.' (K. Odawara)

A Swany in each hand

There are many users who, like me, hold a Swany Bag in each hand for support. Even going up steps, we can pull the bags up alternately one step at a time, and the same for going down. In a wheelchair, I despair when I come to a change in level, and for me the Swany is more valuable than a wheelchair. Here are two actual examples.

'Both my knees have been replaced, and I support myself with a Swany Bag in each hand. I can carry things, too, and my life is a joy now. Thank you so much.' (I. Tokyo)

'With walking sticks, 100 metres was my limit, but with two Swany Bags I find I can now walk as far as I like. This bag is really amazing.' (Y., Funabashi)

Enlarged wheels

In 2013, in response to requests, the 75 mm castor was perfected. We had many requests for larger wheels, and these developed from 45 mm to 50 mm, 60 mm, and 75 mm. We had many requests to change the wheels to 75 mm, but there is one product which cannot be changed to 75 mm.

The Swany Bag has to continue giving support in a confined space such as on the train or plane. If the wheels are any larger than 75 mm, they can collide with each other when changing direction. 100 mm is possible, but the width of the bag would need to be increased, and in a restricted space the bag would no longer offer support for the body. It is a vexing problem, but we would like to respond to the demand for bigger wheels as far as we can.

'I always go everywhere with my Swany Bag. I've been using one for nearly 15 years. The bigger wheels make walking easier. I'm really thankful for it.' (S. Kanazawa)

'With the change to larger wheels, it has become easier to walk, even on bumpy paths. I have three bags, and I choose which one to use depending on what I want to use it for. My Swany goes with me every day.' (N. Tokyo)

Quiet castors

Another request from users is that they want the wheels to be even quieter. Although the castors have become quieter, there are still improvements to be made.

'My Swany combines the roles of bag, trailer and chest of drawers. It's compact, light, and smart-looking. I'd like it if the wheels could be quieter, though.' (K. Kobe)

'I have a disability in my leg. I am more comfortable with the Swany than with a stick. This is my first 75 mm, but I hope that the castors can be made quieter.' (Y. Nagoya)

A lighter bag

Because of the need to maintain the support strength, this is one area where we have not made dramatic progress. I see it as my most important remaining challenge.

'Because I have a disorder of the semicircular canals, which affects my balance, I rely on my Swany wherever I go. I don't have much strength, so I would like it if it could be made a little lighter.' (Y. Tokyo)

'I travel to painting classes by bus and train. My Swany is an ideal companion because it carries all my equipment and supports me too. Couldn't it just be made a little lighter?' (T. Tokyo)

Urgent servicing

At our company, three technicians are on hand to replace wheels or handles, repair tube-connecting pins or carry out other repairs and return the bag within one week. We all take pride in our products being 'not just another bag'. Our telephone contact deals with everything on the spot.

We were told by the people at one shop that a customer, when told that the repair would take one week, told them that it was impossible to walk without it, and insisted on taking another one away. Since then, they have kept a frame for loaning to repair customers.

'Thank you for making my second Swany as good as new again. I can't go out without it. Even my wife takes second place.' (Y, Kobe)

'My repaired Swany came back days sooner than I expected. It was cleaned all over and looks brand new. Thank you so much!' (K, Hirakata)

Requests for future attention

Here are some comments which present further challenges to address in the future.

'I'd like to have a holder for a walking stick or umbrella.' (K. Tokyo)

'I'd like a hook on the handle for hanging a shopping bag.' (H. Tokyo)

'I bought the S size, but actually I'd like something even smaller.' (H. Umeda)

Loyal customers

Shigenobu Ushiro, the manager of the luggage shop Lovely in Osaka, is well known as a self-professed Swany expert. He spends half an hour with each customer exhaustively explaining the various features of the

Swany Bag, and over more than ten years he has built up a detailed record of who bought which model, now containing over a thousand names. His shop is the top seller of Swany Bags in Japan, and they have achieved this position without giving points or discounts, always selling at the full price.

In 2014, Boo Takagi, ukulele player and former member of the rock-comedy band The Drifters, visited us at Swany. Wheeling a Swany Tino Sako, which by then was already out of production, he marvelled at all the different bags he saw. He looked at all the smaller sized bags and ordered the smallest. He is a great Swany user, owning six bags which he chooses from according to the occasion. 'In Hawaii, people are always asking me where I bought my bag,' he told us. We were also delighted to hear that he treats his bags with care, always giving them a thorough wipe clean before taking them out.

In Asia

In 2012, Ms Wong, the owner of the Metro department store in Singapore, came to Japan. While in Tokyo, she noticed the Swany Bag, and, instantly attracted, bought one each for herself and her mother. She continued to buy Swany Bags for shopping and travel.

Subsequently, she started selling Swany Bags at her own department store in Singapore. Although transport costs and import duties make them cost half as much again as in Japan, 10,000 have already been sold, and the Swany is becoming popular among older well-to-do people in Singapore. Our bags are also bought by shoppers from nearby Malaysia and Indonesia.

Swany is now steadily breaking through into the 'Greater China' market of Hong Kong, Taiwan, and continental China.

Troubleshooting meetings

Since 2017, we have been holding 'troubleshooting meetings' for Swany users, and by the end of 2020 we had held 80 meetings, at 13 venues.

One of these meeting places is the Keio department store in Tokyo, where supervisor Hiroki Kawatani hosts meetings with our users. We get requests like, 'The handle won't go down,' 'I can't adjust the height,' and 'The wheels are worn.'

We advise the customers to replace the wheels when they are worn and inform them that there is a model with stoppers. Occasionally, our staff are kept busy until late at night making repairs, and a customer once treated them to a round of sweet bean waffles as a reward for their efforts.

These unique troubleshooting meetings are attracting an increasing number of users all over the country.

Slimmed-down wheelchair

In 2003, my left leg, the good one, started to weaken, and I went to consult the doctors at Shirotori Hospital. They told me that I had post-polio syndrome (PPS), and that I should get a wheelchair immediately. Accordingly, I spent the next three years as a wheelchair user.

I began to have doubts, however, and so I went to see Professor Kyōzō Yonemoto of the Jikei University School of Medicine in Tokyo, an authority on PPS.

At Professor Yonemoto's clinic in Tokyo, there were six or seven other patients, who were all peering into my face. One of them eventually asked me, 'Aren't you the President of Swany?' I was surprised to hear that four of them had Swany Bags. While we were chatting, my turn came, and Professor Yonemoto himself came out and called, 'Mr Miyoshi, please.' Up until then, the nurse had been calling the patients!

The first thing he said was that ever since he heard that the developer of the Swany Bag was coming he had been looking forward to meeting me. It turned out that Professor Yonemoto had been recommending the Swany Bag to his patients.

He then said to me, 'Mr Miyoshi, you can walk, can't you? For as long as you can walk, you mustn't use a wheelchair. Your muscles will weaken if you do.' I was delighted to hear this advice. In all the 15 years since, I have been walking with a Swany Bag in each hand, and I have not used a wheelchair. This is entirely thanks to Professor Yonemoto.

During my three years as a wheelchair user, I found myself constantly bumping into furniture and door frames on account of the wheelchair being too big, and trying to get it into the boot of a taxi was a major challenge. Another problem was not being able to get close enough to the washbasin because of the footrests getting in the way.

In places like France and Poland, I found that I couldn't use a lift designed to take two passengers and had to leave my wheelchair on the ground floor while I went up to a meeting on one of the upper floors. I also once had a puncture in one of the tyres, and tried a bicycle shop, only to find that my Japanese tyres were not compatible, and had to wait four days for a whole new wheel to arrive from Japan.

At the same time, using a wheelchair made me aware of the kindness of others. In Europe or America, if I came to a flight of steps or a stony path, people would immediately come forward and carry me, wheelchair and all, from both sides. Airport staff would tip the wheelchair back with me in it until it was almost horizontal and load me onto the airport bus in a matter of seconds. I have even been carried on board a plane piggyback.

But the experience taught me first-hand the inconvenience felt by the users of wheelchairs that are too bulky, and it aroused in me the ambition to see if I couldn't create a more compact folding wheelchair myself. My three years living with a wheelchair were by no means wasted.

Down to less than half size, 80 years on

I started making drawings of wheelchairs with a reduced width, at home and while travelling. What troubled me for years was the problem of making an X-frame that would not sandwich the seat when folded. I tried making and remaking drawings, but could not find a solution, and the days and months passed.

One day in 2005, on board a plane bound for New York, I took out my graph paper and drew an X-frame with curved, rather than straight, lines to reduce the width, and realised that when the lower half of the curved X-frame was pushed inward to fold it away, the curved upper half would contain enough space to hold the seat without bulging. In this way, by making the arms of the X-frame curved, the width could be reduced by as much as 7 cm. I had passed the first hurdle.

Length down by 30 cm

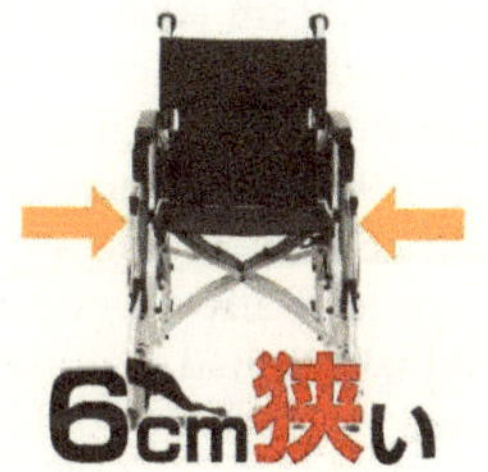

Width when in use
down by 6 cm

Width when folded
down to 22 cm

The next step was to reduce the width of the wheels by housing the brake within the hub. Conventional wheelchairs had the brake tied to the hub, adding to the width. I made several trips to China, a supplier of wheelchairs, and searched for a manufacturer of internal hub brakes. I found a leading maker in Dongguan, and had hubs made with a width of 7 cm, or 3 cm narrower than the commercially available hub, meaning a reduction in width of 6 cm left and right, investing about ¥10 million.

As a result, we achieved a total reduction in width of 13 cm (7 cm with the curved X-frame and 6 cm with the hub brakes), giving us a revolutionary new wheelchair with a folded width of 22 cm instead of the conventional 35 cm.

The next challenge was how to fold away the footrests. The only options were to have them flip up or fold away below. I tried different arrangements but had to eliminate the fold-away option for lack of space.

With the flip-up option, there was the problem of the footrests colliding with surrounding objects above, in front and to the sides. I alternately made drawings of these points of contact and lay in bed thinking, and a series of flashes of inspiration enabled me to take off millimetres at a time until, after a few months, I had managed to get the length down by a whole 30 cm.

With 13 cm taken off the folded width by means of the curved X-frame, and 30 cm taken off the length by means of the flip-up footrests, the volume of the wheelchair when folded was reduced from the 220 litres of the conventional model to 100 litres, or less than half.

In 1933, the American company E&J invented the X-frame, which made it possible to fold a wheelchair into half its size. Eighty years on, in 2014, we at Swany developed a wheelchair that could be folded into a size half of that. We had rewritten wheelchair history!

Two wheelchairs could now easily fit into the boot of a taxi, the user could get close to a washbasin while still in the chair, it could be kept by the door without taking up a lot of space, delivery costs would be reduced and, being 6 cm narrower when in use, the chair could easily pass through most automated ticket gates.

Previous patents

We had to overcome some major hurdles before this revolutionary wheelchair could make its appearance on the market, however. These hurdles were lying in wait for us right up until it went on sale.

In summer 2006, when the chair was on the point of going on sale, we were advised by the Japan Patent Office that a patent for a curved X-frame had previously been filed, and that our patent could not be granted. Ten had already been produced, and the new wheelchair had made its appearance in the media, and now, totally unexpectedly, we found ourselves in a desperate predicament.

We immediately called a management meeting, which concluded that a newcomer to the market could not survive without patent rights. We decided to dispose of the goods already produced and inform the press that we were withdrawing from the market.

It was still a huge disappointment, considering what good news our new compact wheelchair, reduced to half the size of the conventional folding wheelchair after a wait of 80 years, would be to users. So, believing that the most important thing was that it should be made available as soon as possible, I decided to give the commercialisation rights away to a certain leading manufacturer. I visited their office, told them I wanted to offer the new technology free for the benefit of users, and returned, leaving the drawings with them.

But however long I waited, the wheelchair didn't go on sale.

After two years, when my patience was starting to wear thin, a new year greeting card came from the company with an encouraging message. I felt a sense of relief, but still I waited and still nothing happened. It seemed that the President, who did not have a disability, could not see that the reduction in size of the wheelchair would be just as important to users as reduction in weight.

In 2012, feeling that I must realise this ambition come what may, I made my move. I pressed patent attorney Yasushi Toyosu for his advice, and after repeated discussions with him, a new plan emerged, a model that would not conflict with previously filed patents. In technology, just as when building a client base, persistence and a refusal to give up yielded results.

Wheelchairs were far removed from our core business of gloves.

But, happily, the Swany Bag, too, was produced in the same factories as our gloves, mainly in China. The production of wheelchairs involved the same processing of fabric, aluminium and plastics as bags, and we had connections with the fabric, aluminium and plastic industries.

The design belongs to the areas of dynamics and geometry, but in bags and wheelchairs alike, performance depends on factors such as the strength and structure of the component parts. Most importantly, we listened to the conventional wisdom of bag and wheelchair manufacturers and looked for unconventional solutions, leading us finally to the new product.

It was via this circuitous path that in 2014 the Swany Mini wheelchair made its second debut.

A world first! A wheelchair with pockets

Two years after the wheelchair went on sale, we began to receive requests from users for pockets.

I made phone calls to about 40 people, and one of them, Mr Shinji Okumura from Okayama, told me that a pocket for things like keys, glasses and smartphone near the armrest was essential. He wouldn't put the phone down until I agreed.

'At the moment, I have a bag under the seat, and if I need something I have to put my hand down between my legs and open the zip to get it out. It's difficult for me with my weak arms and legs,' he said.

He urged me, 'Mr Miyoshi, you invented the walking bag. People are relying on you to come up with a wheelchair pocket. Come on, it's sure to be a success!'

As a result, the wheelchair now has pockets on both sides, above and to the front of the main wheels and to the side of the armrests.

'With the folded width reduced to an astonishing 22 cm, it can be loaded into the car with ease. It's the most comfortable wheelchair I've ever used, and it's easy for my helper to push.' (S. Tokyo)

'I found I could load it into the back of the car myself. And the tyres are puncture-proof, so there's no need to worry about air.' (S. Tokyo)

'There's more than enough space in the boot of my car for two of them. Using the bathroom is easy. I can keep things in the pockets, and I can enjoy gardening with the footrests folded up.' (M. Aichi)

Our conversation with our wheelchair users continues.

Cartoon appeal

When I heard that Fumi Ueda, who I introduced in the last chapter as our recruitment officer, draws cartoons as a hobby, I asked her if she could draw a cartoon history of the development of the Swany Bag and the Swany Mini. She got drawing straight away and produced an eight-page cartoon.

When we had a visit from a group of elementary school pupils and showed them the cartoons, they went down very well, and the children were much more interested in reading them than in listening to our explanations. Ms Ueda has been very successful in making the rather technical aspects of our story easy to follow, even for girls and boys.

These cartoons are playing their part in our business activities not only in Japan but also overseas in English and Chinese translation, reinforcing Swany's passion for creativity with the power of pictures.

Swany's business today

It's now time to stand back and look at Swany's business now that we have found a path beyond gloves.

A company's performance is shown by its profit-and-loss statements and its balance sheets. The one shows the year's sales and earnings, while the other shows the company's strength at a given time. For each of our divisions, we hold discussions on the outlook for the month end and quarter end based on the profit-and-loss statement and balance sheet and set goals for the safe operation of the business. We also hold all-day conferences twice a month, where we set company policy, and consider the agenda arising from the different divisions.

Yearly turnover between 1980 and 2000 was ¥3 billion to ¥4.5 billion, and between 2000 and 2020 it has been level at ¥4 billion to ¥5 billion. In the second half of this period, turnover from bags has risen to approximately ¥1.2 billion, but gloves have fallen by about the same amount. Fortunately, however, in Japan we became the top producer of gloves in 2018. In addition, we have now maintained our position as No. 1 for skiing gloves for seven years, and ¥1 billion for America can be added to this.

Our glove business looks set to maintain its competitiveness with orders from leading customers, but our competitors in countries like Indonesia and Vietnam are expanding their facilities, and we need to put more effort into improving productivity in high-mix low-volume manufacturing and establishing and maintaining a system of year-round operation. Developing the spring and summer sports market as a response to global warming is another urgent task.

A cause for concern is that our gross profit margin, which until about 2000 had been at least 30%, has since fallen. But if we continue to develop original products, and if our investment in the Swany Ski and Elmer brands in Japan and Europe in 2018 is successful, we should have a chance to recover. And if skiing gloves can make a comeback in America, we can participate in this market as an ODM (original design manufacturer) supplier in Japan.

As for the bag and wheelchair businesses, we should be able to maintain our competitiveness thanks to our innovative four-wheel stopper for stopping swivel castors and our original bag attachment hook, while we look to further improvements in functionality, lightness, and design.

Meanwhile, the Swany Mini wheelchair, which can be folded into half the space of a conventional folding chair and can get up close to a kitchen worktop, has sold about a thousand a year in the small purchasing market. In 2020 it makes its appearance on the rental market, 10 times the size of the purchasing market.

This Swany Mini has enabled us to reach beyond the seasonal glove business and looks set to achieve a high profitability. In addition to its compactness, by saving space for parking and reducing transport costs, it looks likely to become a leading product from the point of view of environmental protection. We have obtained patents in Japan, the United States and China, and our growth into a leading medium-sized enterprise looks assured.

Invitation to the imperial garden party

In 2013, I was awarded the Order of the Rising Sun, Fifth Class, in recognition of the invention of the body-supporting walking bag.

I was invited to the autumn imperial garden party at the Akasaka Imperial Gardens in Tokyo, where members of the imperial family thanked me for my work, and the Emperor himself greeted me with a smile, face-to-face. Empress Michiko, who accompanied the Emperor with her hand in his arm, spoke to me, seeing me leaning on my Swany Bag, saying, 'I hope you're not tired. Please take care of yourself.'

Princess Masako was not present, and the Crown Prince looked as if he might be missing her a little. Prince Akishino and his wife Princess Kiko and their daughter Princess Mako followed, smiling, and then Princesses Akiko and Yōko of Mikasa. Princess Takamado then followed, accompanied by her daughters Tsuguko and Noriko, and, looking at my name badge, called out, 'Oh, Mr Swany!', seeming surprised to see me standing there. Princess Noriko kindly urged me to sit down in my wheelchair. Meeting all these members of the imperial family was quite an overwhelming experience.

Among the other guests, I met the men's figure skating champion Yuzuru Hanyū, and my wife and my youngest daughter Yasuko had their photograph taken with him. Then a lady approached me and said, 'I'm a great Swany fan. Your bags saved my mother. I use one, too. I'm here on behalf of my mother, who couldn't come because of her poor legs.' I was taken aback to find another satisfied customer there.

My disability in my right leg, which caused me such grief that at one point I even wanted to end my life, eventually gave me the impetus to develop the Swany Bag, which helped satisfy the needs of so many people.

Then, having post-polio syndrome pushed me to perfect the Swany Mini, the world's most compact folding wheelchair. And now here I was, meeting members of the imperial family and finding that they knew the name Swany. It was a day for me to take pride in my good fortune.

PART 3.

THE SCIENCE OF FASTING

Drawn to fasting

When I was 43 years old, I caught a cold and went to Shirotori Hospital, where I was told that I had chronic nephritis, a serious kidney condition, and needed immediate hospitalisation.

While I was in hospital, my elder brother Yoriaki sent me a copy of *The Science of Fasting* by Dr Mitsuo Kōda. According to this book, fasting and light eating can enhance circulation and bring about improvement in various illnesses, and I read it, intrigued by the author's persuasive argument.

It seemed that Dr Kōda had always had a sweet tooth, and grew up eating large quantities of *zenzai*, a snack of sugar-sweetened azuki beans with rice dumplings. He began to suffer damage to multiple organs, and eventually succumbed to chronic gastrointestinal and liver disease. He studied medicine at Osaka University and underwent treatment for his own condition but showed no sign of recovering. He then tried the 'Nishi health system' devised by Katsuzō Nishi. While following this regime, he found the yearning for sugar so strong that he binged on various sweet snacks, not caring if it killed him. This painful experience finally led him to the idea of fasting.

The author talked about the Buddhist teaching of emancipation from afflictions or negative emotions. All of us suffer from afflictions every day of our lives. As a businessperson, I knew that the world of business was an arena of life-and-death struggle, which naturally gave rise to afflictions. Why not give fasting a try, I thought. Fasting was a spiritual discipline practised by ascetics and holy men like Gandhi. It might even help my kidney problem!

A curious fasting 'camp'

The 'Kōda Clinic' I visited was truly a strange hospital. Medicines were described as 'poisons' and none was prescribed. There were no nurses, and the sharp smell of disinfectant was conspicuous by its absence. The only people were Dr Kōda, a clinic manager, a nutritionist, and the food preparation staff. There were stories of cancer patients who had survived, balding men whose hair had grown back, and school students with muscular dystrophy taking part in sports day events.

The patients didn't look like ordinary hospital patients, either. The atmosphere was more akin to that of a sports club training camp. In the central hall, about 36 m² in area, there were about 20 people, some swinging their bodies like the pendulum of a clock, others shaking with their arms stretched up towards the sky. This must be the 'Nishi-shiki gymnastics,' I thought.

'What's your trouble?' I asked them. One replied, 'I suffer terribly from rheumatism.' Another said, simply, 'Cancer.' All of them had been told that modern medicine could not cure their diseases.

To the left side of the hall was the 'Kōda garden', a small plot of land with green leafy vegetables growing luxuriantly. These were the source of the raw vegetable juice that formed the basis of our diet.

Expelling impacted stool

Lunch on my first day was a half bowl of brown rice gruel and about 200 g of tofu. 'Is this all?' I thought. Just brown rice and tofu, with only natural salt for seasoning, was far from the things I was used to eating. To be honest, I couldn't stand it. But after a few days I started to get used to it, and, perhaps because of my hunger, I began to find it palatable.

After about one week, I embarked on the 11-day 'clear soup fast'. Breakfast was a small glass of vegetable juice made from greens such as spinach and lettuce, about 180 ml. For lunch and dinner, I had about the same amount of clear soup, which consisted of thin fish stock flavoured with a little soy sauce and brown sugar. In addition to this I drank about 1.8 litres of water and persimmon leaf tea with vitamins intermittently throughout the day. All this came to a total of 150 kcal per day.

Twice each day I felt the urge to defecate, and each time I expelled a small amount of brown, sandy impacted stool. Over a few days I estimated that the amount expelled would add up to about half a washbasin full. The others had all produced about half a bucketful, and Dr Kōda told me that I had still only lost about a third. Impacted stool is retained faeces that accumulates as a result of continued eating over and above the amount of food digested. Gases from impacted stool in the gastrointestinal tract invade the body via the blood vessels, causing a multitude of diseases, it is said.

Even after four days, the introductory 'clear soup fast' was easier than I had imagined, and I was keen to lose all my impacted stool. 'Doctor, I could do this for 15, no, 20 days,' I said. 'It's easy because you're taking salt,' he replied. 'Why not try the "strict fast" for two days?'

After starting the strict fast, which allowed only water and persimmon tea, I lost courage. Just lifting my body up was burdensome. I could just manage to read a book. Cutting out salt and sugar was tough. Not lifting a pair of chopsticks once all day, the time seemed endless, and I could hardly bear it.

I carried on reading books from morning till night, trying to suppress my rumbling stomach. After nine days had passed, Dr Kōda announced, 'The day after tomorrow you'll be having brown rice.' When he said that, my stomach started to groan. I imagined I could detect the smell of curry or fried rice cooking. Visions of my favourite dishes appeared and disappeared, only to appear again: chicken-and-egg rice, tempura with noodles. For the next two days, I couldn't think about anything except eating. My craving for food was driving me mad. Then, after 11 days, at long last my fast came to an end.

'I've done it,' I said to myself, and gave myself a cheer.

I am of small build to begin with, and after my fast my weight went down 10 kg to 43 kg. The doctor was very careful about my return to eating, perhaps because of concern about the risk of twisted bowel. I started on brown rice gruel (one part rice to 20 parts water, rising to one part rice to 10 parts water). 'Doctor, I'm starving! I can't stand it!' I cried out, but the doctor pointed out that my weight was going up half a kilo a day. 'You've been eating too much all this time,' he said.

Over four days, I gradually progressed to eating ordinary cooked rice, with a calorie intake of 1650 kcal a day. Breakfast was just 180 ml of vegetable juice (50 kcal), and at lunch and dinner I ate brown rice with raw seasonal vegetables, some grilled fish, tofu, and seaweed (800 kcal each meal). To me this seemed like a banquet. Nothing makes human beings feel as humble as hunger. Seeing all this food made me think of all the starving children there are on this planet.

I was so hungry I couldn't wait for mealtimes. During my 33 days there, I ate the equivalent of only about seven days' worth of a standard diet, but thanks to the reduction in impacted stool my gastrointestinal absorption improved and, by the time I left, my weight had recovered to 47 kg.

Before every meal, I now recite these verses by Sumiko Deguchi, the second spiritual leader of Oomoto.

The blessings of heaven and earth have made this food / let me not waste a single vegetable leaf
In a single grain of rice dwell the spirits of fire, water and soil / let me never forget this
The blessing of fire, water and soil / this is the true form of the spirit of heaven and earth.

Busy clinic routine

While I was at the clinic, my day began at five o'clock when I heard the beep of my wristwatch, which was my signal to get up. I put away my bedclothes and proceeded to the washroom and exchanged greetings with the other patients.

Returning to my bed, I knelt facing the direction of the Oomoto sanctuary in Ayabe and recited the Oomoto prayer. I gave thanks for the experience of fasting and prayed as usual for the fellowship of people of all religions, nations, and languages.

Every day I took 40 cc of Suimag, a natural laxative derived from sea salt, dissolved in a glass of water, not as a medicine but to promote the removal of my impacted stool.

Between 5.30 and 6.00, we did 'naked therapy'. With the windows wide open, we exposed our skin to the fresh air, went under the blankets, and then exposed our bodies again. We repeated this, gradually increasing the time spent uncovered. This was to strengthen our skin and to expel accumulated carbon monoxide, and if practised daily it is said that it can contribute to the treatment of cancer.

The doctor also instructed me to do Nishi-shiki gymnastics, which I still spend an hour doing every day, wearing casual clothes. These consist of the following:

1   'Goldfish' exercise, 200 times: abdominal muscle exercises performed facing upwards, folding the hands behind the neck, and moving like a fish swimming.
2   Capillary exercise, two minutes: facing upwards, raising one's arms and legs perpendicularly and shaking them.
3   Exercise with palms and soles joined, 200 times: facing upwards, with palms and soles joined, stretching and contracting arms and legs together.
4   Dorsoventral exercise, 200 times: kneeling with legs apart and hands clasped behind, swinging the trunk to left and right.
5   Eleven neck exercises, 20 times each: turning the neck left, right, forward, backward, clockwise, and anticlockwise.

Dr Kōda told me to repeat this sequence of five exercises, which takes about 20 minutes, a few times. It took quite a lot of energy, but afterwards I felt recharged and revitalised.

The manager showed me my bed, explaining that I needed a flat bed to straighten my spine. I couldn't quite believe that I was being given such a hard bed to lie on: under a mat only a centimetre thick was a plywood panel.

Lying on this bed straightened the back, promoting liver, kidney, and intestinal function, I was told. But I found it so uncomfortable I couldn't sleep at all, so although I lay on it like this for reading during the day, at night I used three of the thin mats. Mercifully, at least the bed cover was soft and comfortable.

Then I had another surprise: the pillow. 'It takes a little getting used to,' the manager told me, and showed me a semicircular wooden pillow. Sleeping with my neck resting on the curved surface would improve my circulation, my head would be kept cooler than my feet, my cervical vertebrae would be straightened, and I would sleep soundly, the manager explained. It took me a whole month to get used to this hard wooden pillow.

After dinner, we all looked forward to the hot-and-cold bath. We submerged ourselves up to the neck for one minute in the natural underground water, which was a year-round 15 degrees, followed by a minute bathing in hot water. We alternated, bathing five times in cold and four times in hot water, finishing with cold. This hot-and-cold bathing gave a boost to our circulation, and relieved our tiredness, and was most pleasant. This can be easily imagined by anyone familiar with the sauna, which is based on a similar principle.

At Dr Kōda's clinic, I read 40 volumes of *Stories of the Spiritual World* by Onisaburo Deguchi, as well as books by Dr Kōda and by the Buddhist author Daisaku Ikeda, and other books about Christianity, Buddhism, and other religions, as well as Gandhi's writings on health – 55 volumes in all. It was an unusually fulfilling time for me.

My companion, the university student

We slept two to a room, and my roommate was a student studying literature at Kyoto University. For 33 days, while reading my books, I wondered how I could best encourage him.

I often asked him to help me read a difficult character in the book I was reading, and he always obliged, but he had little willpower. While we were fasting, he used to turn the pages of cookery books and gaze at the photographs of yakitori and tempura all day long.

He was there to try to cure stomach ulcers and intestinal catarrh, but he used to slip out when Dr Kōda wasn't looking to buy cakes. He tried to tempt me once by offering me one. 'What? Do you want to kill me?' I said, raising my voice, and he wolfed his cakes down in a hurry. Sure enough, the next morning he had severe diarrhoea.

If you don't have the will to see something through to the end, you won't get any help from Heaven. When I checked out, I left this note for my roommate: 'Don't presume upon others' indulgence, not society's, not Dr Kōda's, not your parents'. You're a good, intelligent young man. You can do it!' I wonder how he's getting on now. Hang in there, my friend!

Learning from morning assembly

Every morning, come rain or come hail, we gathered at 7.30 for morning assembly. It was like a university class, with people taking notes in their notebooks and making tape recordings.

All 24 of us put our hands together in an attitude of prayer and chanted the five verses recited by Buddhist monks before meals, vowing to adhere to the strict diet. Dr Kōda then asked if anyone was having any difficulties. After this, he started to deliver a lecture on food: 'Brown rice contains 15.5% water, 6.8% protein...'

Brown rice is the king of foods, he explained. As much as 95% of the vitamins and minerals in rice are contained in the bran and germ.

Compared with white rice, brown rice has twice the ash, calcium, and phosphorus, 2.3 times the potassium and fats, three times the fibre and iron, and four times the vitamin B1 and B2. Muscovado sugar contains between three and ninety times the ash, sodium, calcium, phosphorus, and iron as white sugar.

Iron is needed in significant quantities by the body for growth, and the body needs one gram of calcium per day. Potassium is important for excretion of waste from the liver, and vitamin B1 is essential for the prevention of diabetes. Vitamin B2 prevents skin problems and sodium is essential for maintenance of life. Phosphorus is important to bones and teeth, we learned.

We were also taught to use natural sun-dried sea salt or rock salt, which are rich in calcium, manganese, and iron. Apparently even clams cannot survive in a solution of refined sodium chloride.

White sugar is a calcium thief and should be avoided. An adult should take no more than 30 grams a day, but up to 90 grams of muscovado may be eaten safely, and 100 grams of honey may be eaten without any of the harm associated with sugar.

Learning from the patients

After the doctor's talk, the patients spoke about their experiences.

One morning, Kinnosuke Muraji, a 65-year-old man, spoke.

Mr Muraji had been troubled by rheumatism and high blood pressure for seven years, and after 17 days of a raw vegetable diet he lost his impacted stool. His blood pressure improved dramatically, his systolic pressure going down from 198 to 143, and his diastolic pressure from 125 to 93. His visual acuity also recovered from 0.2 (or 20/100) to 0.8 (or 20/25).

Some days later, I heard the story of Hisami Shimamoto, whose skin had turned white from childhood because of vitiligo, and who had visited university hospitals one after another. Late one night, she overheard her parents talking about her in the next room, worried that she would never find a husband with her skin condition. At hospital, she had her photograph taken naked in front of the interns and nurses, which left her in tears. She had come here because she had heard of someone recovering from vitiligo by following a raw vegetable diet. I could really sympathise with her, having had a similar experience in my own childhood, and her story brought tears to my eyes.

Seventy-seven-year-old Yoshiko Kawamura said that after 55 days of following a raw vegetable diet a black hair, one centimetre long, had sprouted in the middle of her white hair, and Dr Kōda came and took a photograph of it. Our morning assemblies were full of astonishing stories like this.

Michiaki Fujita, an elementary school teacher, described himself as a 'walking textbook of diseases'. He had come from Osaka, having been referred to Dr Kōda. During his third fast, he announced that he had produced 70 pieces the shape and size of a quail's egg in his stool. These had been lodged in his intestinal wall and had been preventing him from absorbing nutrients. I still remember the smile on his face as he said that he felt healthy for the first time in his life, having got rid of this impacted stool.

I also heard a story told by Sōichirō Musha, a university professor following a raw vegetable diet to treat his bladder cancer. Apparently, many mountain climbers drink sterile urine to increase their white blood cells, to kill pathogens and to cleanse the blood. This came as a complete surprise to me.

Every morning, after assembly, all 24 of us performed 15 Nishi-shiki exercises for one hour.

Nephritis cured by a raw vegetable diet

When I left the clinic, Dr Kōda gave me his seal of approval, saying that my nephritis could be cured by a raw vegetable diet. Arriving back home, I put it into practice straight away. For breakfast, I made a juice of raw seasonal vegetables in the mixer with a little water added. For lunch and dinner, I had a raw salad, with brown rice flour, radish, carrot, yam, and 4 g of natural sea salt. One meal contained 500 kcal, and with 50 kcal for my morning juice my intake came to 1050 kcal.

At lunch and dinner, I drank 250 g of vegetable juice, and spooned 70 g of brown rice flour into my mouth. It wasn't delicious, but it had a certain flavour. I had 120 g of grated carrot, 100 g of grated radish, and 30 g of grated yam, with 4 g of natural salt sprinkled on it. It really was just like eating rabbit food, a seriously ascetic diet. My father, who had cheerfully endured spending a week at a time sleeping on night trains, joined me, saying, 'If it's that good for you I'll try it myself,' but after just three days he threw in the towel.

A plate of grated radish without a nice piece of grilled mackerel to go with it was decidedly unappetising. Faced with 120 g of grated carrot, my stomach groaned in protest. The yam sprinkled with salt, however, was a nice flavour which I was familiar with, and the vegetable juice tasted as always.

While keeping up this diet, I visited the local Kamada Clinic to check for blood and protein in my urine, and I reported the results to Dr Kōda every month. One, two, three months went by and still there was no im-

provement. I appealed to Dr Kōda, telling him I was at the end of my te-
ther, but he encouraged me to keep going for a few more months. Just as
he had predicted, after six months my urine blood and protein levels started to go down. I kept going, and after nine months my nephritis had
completely gone.

'Hallelujah!' I cried out.

I had done it, although in the process my weight had gone down to 40
kg. Dr Kōda had said to me that it would be better not to mention my diet
to the hospital doctors as they wouldn't understand, but I was so pleased
with myself that I told them anyway. When I started telling the doctor
about my nine-month raw vegetable regimen, he immediately dismissed
it, saying that it had nothing to do with my recovery. A few years later that
doctor died from lung cancer, while still young.

No more than 2,000 kcal per day

Thirty-eight years have passed since my experience of fasting therapy.

Today, my breakfast consists of the juice of one carrot plus one carton
of Ito En 'Daily Vegetable Juice' and, although strictly speaking it's not
allowed, one slice of brown rice bread.

For lunch and dinner, I have a bowl of steamed brown rice with tofu
or beans, small fish such as smelt that can be eaten whole, seaweed, and
vegetables, including root vegetables. I try not to eat anything that doesn't
come under one of these five categories. These two meals provide me with
about 1,600 kcal, and with my breakfast of brown rice bread and juice I
have a daily intake of about 1,800 kcal.

It's easy to cook delicious brown rice in a pressure cooker if you soak
it in water for about three hours first. If you adhere to this five-category
diet, your bowel movements are comfortable and you feel healthy, but if
you eat too much, or the wrong kinds of food, and if you don't try to stay
healthy with whole-body exercise, you're likely to be troubled by lingering
disorders of the eyes, nose, and ears.

The more animal protein you eat, including fish, the darker, the
smellier, the stickier and the harder to pass your stool becomes, leading to
disorders of the organs. Meat, in particular, should be avoided as it makes
the blood cloudy, we are told.

Dr Kōda was at pains to emphasise the importance of not overeating,
saying that keeping your calorie intake to within 2,000 kcal per day should
keep you healthy. Allowing your stomach to empty will enable your
body's cells to exert a pull on the blood, improving circulation. This idea
seems at odds with the model of the heart as a pump, but he explains that
the heart has about as much power as a household sewing machine, and
that it is mechanically impossible to pump the blood to 60 trillion cells in
20 seconds with just a quarter of a horsepower.

Blood flows from the body when it is injured in an accident, but no blood flows from the body of a person who has died of natural causes, Dr Kōda goes on. When alive, the blood is pulled into the cells, it just can't be seen. Even an amoeba, which has no heart, has circulation. The cardiac pump theory fails to explain the fact that sinusitis and otitis media can be cured by fasting, he adds.

The cardiac pump theory, according to which the blood leaves the heart, circulates round the body, and returns to the heart, was proposed by the Englishman William Harvey. In his book *Fasting and Light Eating for Health*, Dr Kōda writes, 'This idea comes from a feudal, autocratic world view, which, laughably, is still blindly adhered to by many physicians even today.'

Dr Kōda told me that he had addressed an open letter to the medical establishment but had received no reply. At the same time, however, Dr Kōda praises Western medicine for its ability to measure things like blood pressure and blood glucose.

In 2015, after having kept up the light eating diet and Nishi-shiki exercises, I visited Sanuki Municipal Hospital for a health check-up. I got full marks in all five indices: my waist circumference was 70 cm, my blood pressure was 93/60, my triglycerides were 39, my HDL cholesterol was 96, and my fasting blood glucose was 86. The doctor was so pleased with me that she suggested that I should give lectures to tell people about my diet and exercises.

A light diet based on love and compassion

My 33 days' stay at Dr Kōda's clinic cost me a mere ¥90,000. This may not seem too surprising, since I was sleeping on a plywood board with a wafer-thin mattress on top and I wasn't being served expensive meals. But it doesn't seem right that I couldn't use my health insurance, although it was there that I had my most successful therapy!

There are some people who can't get on with brown rice, but they can mill their own rice and eat the milled white rice, and then, separately, toast the bran in a frying pan, turning off the heat when the bran changes to a brown colour. This toasted bran can then be taken with vegetable juice, about three tablespoons per day. This will have the same effect as eating brown rice. I have been a devotee of this toasted rice bran for five years now.

Dr Kōda used to joke with his patients that if everyone followed the Nishi-shiki exercise regime, most doctors and pharmacists would go out of business. He also said that he had treated more than 2,000 cancer patients with fasting and a raw vegetable diet, although when the cancer cells exceeded 70% of the affected site the patient couldn't be cured. When I think about his results, even with diseases regarded as incurable by mo dern medicine, I can't help wondering if the more than ¥40 trillion spent annually on healthcare couldn't be reduced.

Recently, we have started hearing warnings about therapies that neglect preventive medicine, treating only the symptoms, life-prolonging treatment for end-of-life patients, and organ transplantation from donors judged to be brain dead. The documentary *Hard to Believe* directed and produced by the American Ken Stone, is a shocking film about the harvesting of organs for transplant.

When he was young, Dr Kōda's own painful experiences made him stop overeating. He saw that, in his words, 'to eat lightly is to cherish all life.' This practice of love and compassion became his life's goal, and he spent the next 50 years sharing his fasting philosophy.

Further, pointing out that a cow eats ten times its own weight of grain, and a yellowtail eats seven times its own weight in sardines, he repeatedly made the case for abstaining from such luxury foods and eating grains and sardines instead for the sake of the environment.

Only the other day I listened to an interview with the late Dr Kōda on the NHK radio programme *Radio Night Flight*. I was moved to hear the voice of the man who had saved me all those years ago. My life has taken a miraculous turn since the time when I was suffering from nephritis.

Most people, hearing the word 'fast' are horrified, but now I can eat ice cream, and I enjoy fruit after lunch and a mid-afternoon snack.

PART 4.

A FUTURE WORLD LANGUAGE

Can English truly be a common language?

The recent novel *In Pleasure* by Mariko Hayashi contains the following passage.

The protagonist, Kusaka, declares:

> « Vous savez, je pense que dans cent ans, il n'y aura plus de langue japonaise. »
>
> 'You know, I think in a hundred years' time there won't be any Japanese language.'
>
> 'No Japanese? I wonder...'
>
> Natsuko tilted her head to one side.
>
> 'Our language disappearing – that would mean the country itself wouldn't exist any longer. I don't think that will happen to Japan.'
>
> 'I'd like to think not, too, but in a hundred years' time Japanese and Japan will both be gone.'
>
> 'I wonder...'
>
> 'It's sad, but I think it'll happen. You can't get a job at a major company if you're not good at English. They've already started teaching English at elementary school. Sooner or later, English will become the official language in Japan. And the way things are going, the country itself won't survive much longer.'

After the environmental crisis, another big problem facing us is that of a common language. Is it really a good idea to give this status to a language from just one part of the world, a difficult language with seven different ways of pronouncing the letter 'a', a complicated language whose textbooks are nearly all taken up with explaining the exceptions to the rules?

If we do, we will be walking into a trap designed to maintain Anglo-American privilege.

Dutch, the 'world' language that came to Japan in the Edo Period before English did, is now in danger of disappearing. If you go to Schiphol Airport in Amsterdam today, you will notice that all the signs are now in English.

It is estimated that of about 8,000 languages now spoken in the world, one is being lost every two weeks. In a hundred years' time, Japanese too could well disappear.

In the European Union, there are few opportunities for politicians who do not speak English, and people of integrity and wisdom are being marginalised. Simmering resentment at this will boil over one day.

Japan is inundated with English neologisms. To take a few examples from the coronavirus pandemic, we hear people debate whether we should 'go to (travel)' to help the economy or 'stay home' to be safe.

People talk about 'social distance', and 'overshoot'. All these words and phrases are pure English. It's totally out of control! I sometimes wonder what country I'm living in. The discussion about the possibility of Japan and the Japanese language disappearing in Hayashi's novel is quite convincing.

The spreading Anglicisation of the world will lead to the extinction of thousands of languages and their cultures.

How can we resist this huge impoverishment and injustice?

Learning Esperanto

I first became aware of the international language Esperanto in 1965, when I read the book *My Travels in Esperanto-land* by Kyotaro Deguchi of Oomoto. In his book, Mr Deguchi describes his experience attending the World Esperanto Congress in Sofia, Bulgaria, and going on to travel around the world for six months using only Esperanto.

I was struck to read how, after Mr Deguchi had prepared himself by shutting himself away in his room and studying for 100 days, he entered the Congress international speech contest, and won second prize. I read this at the time when I was struggling to learn English.

I remained curious about Esperanto, thinking I would like to learn it one day, but I was busy learning Korean and English, and I ended up putting it off for 30 years. I finally started at the age of 55, when my powers of memory were already starting to wane. I took out a subscription to the monthly magazine *Esperanto* published by the Universal Esperanto Association, and, although I wasn't sure how to pronounce the letters of the alphabet, I went through the articles, looking up every word in the dictionary and writing the meaning in the space between the lines with my fibre-tip pen. But before I had finished looking up all the words, the next month's issue would arrive. I redoubled my efforts, getting up at four o'clock every morning and spending two hours studying. For the first year it was like a race to keep up, but then it started to get easier, and after another year I had caught up. I found that I could remember even difficult words after looking them up about 20 or 30 times, and although most of the words were new to me, about two thirds were similar to English but with different endings, and so memorising them was easier than I had expected.

After this, I invited Mr and Ms Sutton of the New Zealand Esperanto Association to stay and practice conversation with me every evening from seven till ten. I invited others, too, from all over the world, to come to Japan and help me with my study, and this continued for about 20 years, until 2016.

I also corresponded with hundreds of Esperanto speakers from all over the world by email, but I let my teachers do the typing for me, so I ended up not being good at writing, although I could speak.

At the World Federalist Congress

Oomoto has adopted the slogan 'One God, one world, one international language'.

'One God' means cooperation between different faiths, and to this end Oomoto was instrumental in launching the Interreligious Gathering of Prayer for World Peace, which has been held on Mt Hiei near Kyoto for the last 30 years.

'One world' refers to the movement for a world federation, with the countries of the world united under a single government, as proposed following the end of World War II by Einstein, Schweitzer, and others – something like the European Union but on a world scale. For many years, the world federation movement in Japan was spearheaded by the Nobel prize-winning physicist Hideki Yukawa. 'World federation is yesterday's dream and tomorrow's reality. Today is the step from yesterday to tomorrow,' he declared.

In line with 'one international language' Oomoto has been involved in the Esperanto movement since the 1920s, and during the pre-war period half of its resources were spent on international activities.

In 2002, the 24th Congress of the World Federalist Movement was held in London, with 250 delegates from 36 countries, one of whom was me. At the Esperanto sectional meeting, Professor Ron Glossop of Southern Illinois University gave the keynote speech, in which he said:

There are a constant 700,000 people from Europe studying English in the UK, and the money spent annually in the EU as a whole on English learning is a staggering €17 billion (about ¥2.5 trillion). In Brussels, home of the EU headquarters, the job advertisements in the newspapers have the condition 'English required', and, further down, in small print, they add, 'Applicants must have English to native language standard.' Demanding English at native speaker level means that the majority of people are unfairly discriminated against. The world federation movement will only make a breakthrough by allying itself with Esperanto.

Objections came back from his listeners: 'But Esperanto doesn't have any culture!' 'You can't express emotions in an artificial language!' 'You can't write literature in it!'

David Kelso of the Esperanto Association of Britain answered, 'There are thousands of children born to Esperanto-speaking couples, who are bilingual in Esperanto and the language of the country where they live. It's a fact that they have nurtured an Esperanto culture. Tens of thousands of works of literature have been translated and published in Esperanto, and there are tens of thousands of books originally written in Esperanto, as well as hundreds of magazines.'

An Italian federalist then stood up to speak. 'A man-made language is useless,' he said. Another Esperanto speaker responded, 'English, German, and other languages were all made by humans, our ancestors! The Esperanto alphabet has 28 letters, which are always pronounced the same. The grammar has just 16 basic rules, and unlike English there are no exceptions. A European can learn it in just a tenth of the time needed to learn English, and there are already a million people using Esperanto around the world. It's the most sophisticated of all the world's languages!'

An American delegate, who was working for the World Bank, spoke up, 'Are you telling us we've all got to learn this Esperanto? You must be joking!'

After a lively debate, a resolution was adopted, to the effect that 'World federalists recommend the study of Esperanto, a non-national language,' and this resolution was shown on the World Federalist Movement website.

Newspaper advertisements in EU member states

I wondered for a long time if there wasn't some way of spreading the word about Esperanto.

In 1985, Masao Ogura, the President of Yamato Transport, frustrated by the refusal of the then Ministry of Transport to recognise his company's home delivery service, decided to place full-page advertisements in the national newspapers urging the Ministry to change its stance. This was a direct and public challenge, which generated a lot of support among consumers and other businesses, and eventually the Ministry of Transport had to give in and allow home delivery. The advertisements brought about a big change in Japanese society.

Every year since 1992 I have attended the World Esperanto Congress, held in a different world city each year, and I have often heard the view expressed that the future of Esperanto depends on the European Union. Remembering the Yamato Transport advertising campaign, I had the idea of taking the same approach to the EU.

I could place a full-page advertisement in European newspapers, I thought, and I sought help and advice from Esperanto organisations in EU countries. First, in 2002, with the cooperation of the President of the European Esperanto Union, I placed an advertisement in two Belgian newspapers, and one of them, the *Metro*, printed it not as an advertisement but as a full-page article, with the headline 'English can't solve the EU's language problem'. Lode, my Esperanto tutor, who was back in Belgium at the time, was grinning from ear to ear when I saw him.

The following year, I placed an advertisement in the Italian daily *La Repubblica*. Immediately after it appeared, six members of the Italian Parliament announced that they would take up the language problem with the EU. The radio station Radio Deejay broadcast the full text on its national programme twice. Several thousand people visited the Italian Esperanto Federation's website, and 33 new members were born.

In 2004, it was the turn of the Polish newspaper *Rzeczpospolita*. Roman Dobrzyński, a director working for Polish Television, interviewed me, and here too, thanks to the newspaper's goodwill, the 'advertisement' appeared as an ordinary article. They told me that they had come to see Esperanto in a new light, as making a contribution to world peace rather than being just a hobby.

In the same year, I placed an advertisement in the French *Le Monde*, and in the next year my advertisement appeared in 25 newspapers in 13 countries, including the German *Die Zeit*, the Belgian *La Libre Belgique*, the Lithuanian *Lietuvos rytas*, and newspapers in Slovakia, Estonia, Latvia, the Czech Republic, Hungary, and Slovenia.

But my brother Yoriaki, who helped with drafting the advertisement, told me that the effect was just a drop in the ocean. At the time, I was reading the novel *Genghis Khan* serialised in the *Nikkei* newspaper, and I came to the passage where Genghis Khan broke through the Great Wall of China by concentrating his whole army of 200,000 at a point where there were few lookouts and opening a path five metres wide for his horses to pass through in just three days, thus enabling his invasion of China. 'I should follow Genghis Khan's example,' I decided. Turning my focus on France, I started to concentrate my advertisements on *Le Monde*.

In the two weeks after I placed my tenth advertisement in *Le Monde*, the French Esperanto Union reported 2,300 visits to its website and 7,000 page views. There was an increase in radio programmes discussing language problems, and some 30 new people took up Esperanto in the space of a few weeks.

I asked the grandson of Dr Zamenhof, the creator of Esperanto, who was living in Paris, if he would appear in the newspaper, but I didn't get a reply straight away. While I was waiting, my advertising funds dried up.

My funds had come from about 1,650 m² of land that had originally belonged to Swany, but I had given half of it to my son-in-law and Swany Senior Executive Director Yasunobu Kawakita. I discussed the situation with him, and he disposed of half of his land so that the proceeds could go towards the advertising campaign. This materialised as a two-page advertisement, which I chose to place on 15 December 2010, Zamenhof's birthday. The right-hand page consisted of an interview with Zamenhof's grandson.

At the top of the advertisement was the heading 'Four native Esperanto speakers' with their photographs, names, and countries of origin.

Below this, I quoted from a lecture given to the European Parliament by Professor Reinhard Selten, a recipient of the Nobel Memorial Prize in Economic Sciences, in which he said that the language problems of the EU could not be resolved by the dominance of one national language, and that the neutral and easy-to-learn Esperanto was the most suitable solution. I also mentioned the endeavours of Inazō Nitobe, Under-Secretary General of the League of Nations, and lastly, I wrote about my own reasons for this campaign.

This advertisement had significant results in the new year. Some tens of members of the French Parliament lobbied the EU, with the result that a symposium was held in Paris attended by more than 100 parliamentarians, at which there was lively discussion about Esperanto, while debate about the problems of a common language continued in the media.

Language debate in Warsaw

In 2004, I sponsored a debate about language in Poland, the birthplace of Zamenhof. Four MEPs, eight national parliamentarians and 54 Esperantists took part.

At the party after the language debate in Warsaw, 2004

Barbara Pietrzak of the Esperanto section of Radio Poland secured the participation of Bronislaw Geremek, a former minister of foreign affairs, who was later viewed as a strong candidate for the first President of the European Council.

Ms Pietrzak told me that since this eminent person would be attending, I should pay him a courtesy visit in advance. A date was fixed and my flight from Japan was booked, but before the suggested meeting could take place Dr Geremek pulled out. 'After much thought, I've come to the conclusion that Esperanto can't compete with English, and meeting you won't change my mind,' he explained. This was a big disappointment.

As the sponsor of the debate, I was the first to speak.

I spoke about how in 1921, Inazō Nitobe from Japan, Under-Secretary General of the League of Nations, attended the World Esperanto Congress in Prague, together with more than 2,000 participants from 70 countries, staying for one week. Seeing the potential of Esperanto as a common language, he began lobbying for Esperanto education in the more than 40 member states of the League at the time but failed because of opposition from France.

I also spoke about how Indonesia, a country with more than 700 languages, had succeeded through the education system in establishing Indonesian, based on the Malay language, as a common language, so that the people of the various islands became bilingual in their local language and the common language, and how Indonesia could serve as a model for our goal of making the world's people bilingual in their own national language and a common world language.

The next person to speak was Zamenhof's grandson, who had come from Paris.

'As a specialist in concrete, I have supervised projects in many parts of the world. When the Akashi Kaikyō Bridge was built in Japan, I was invited to give a talk by the Japanese Ministry of Transport. I was pleased to see my audience nodding while they listened to me. However, when I spoke to them individually at the reception that followed, I realised that many of them had not been able to follow my English. It is doubtful that English can really serve as an international language. Esperanto, the language my grandfather created, can be learned easily and is not liable to misunderstanding. The idea is that we use Esperanto as a common language, while in our own countries we use our own local languages.'

Next, Professor Selten, recipient of the Nobel Memorial Prize in Economic Sciences, who had come from Frankfurt, spoke.

'A new age is here, an age of upheaval, when former Eastern Bloc countries like the Czech Republic, Romania and Hungary are joining the EU. The Berlin Wall has collapsed, something we didn't believe we would see. At such a time, we must try to stop the imposition of English, the language of just one region, on the whole human race. And we can achieve this. We should introduce the teaching of Esperanto in the world's schools, as I urged in the European Parliament in 2001.'

Next, a message from Seán Ó Riain, President of the European Esperanto Union, was read out.
'The EU Charter calls for linguistic equality. The promotion of English without any debate is clearly at odds with democracy and justice. It is unconstitutional, and as such we strongly protest.'

The last to speak was Professor Renato Corsetti from Rome, President of the World Esperanto Association.
'The present situation, where people from the Anglosphere enjoy an advantage while those from other nations face discrimination, is unacceptable. The negation of our histories and cultures by English linguistic imperialism must be resisted,' he concluded.
A consensus was reached, which led to the formation of a parliamentary group for the promotion of Esperanto.

Language debate in the European Parliament

Meanwhile, Dr Geremek from Poland, who turned down my request for a meeting, had not completely given up on Esperanto. Later, in 2008, as a deputy speaker of the European Parliament, he invited all MEPs to a debate to discuss whether Esperanto is 'the friend or the enemy of multilingualism', noting that there were 160 MEPs who were in favour of the adoption of Esperanto as an official language, or more than 20%.
I heard that he also read my advertisements in *Le Monde* and commented approvingly on my engagement with the European language issue.
He had taken the lead in organising the meeting, but, tragically, on the day before it was due to take place, Dr Geremek died in a traffic accident on his way to Warsaw Airport. His death was a huge shock to me and to the Esperanto world.

Interrupted lecture tour in France

In 2010, I addressed a series of meetings in nine French cities including Paris, Lyon, and Marseille.
In Paris, an audience of about 40 Esperanto speakers listened attentively to my speech.
They urged me to appeal by mail, fax or whatever means possible to *Le Monde*, where I had been placing my advertisements, to report on the question of a common language for the EU. Although the other French

media frequently took up language matters, *Le Monde* had not published a single article about it.

The next day, in Vannes in the west of France, about 50 people came to hear me speak, but after the meeting I suddenly felt unwell. I felt cold and couldn't sleep and had trouble breathing. I put through a telephone call to my wife, and she told me, 'Esperanto is your life's work, isn't it? You mustn't come back yet' and hung up.

In the end, I was helped back to Paris by Atilio, a local Esperanto teacher, and eventually made it back to Japan, now gasping for breath. Fortunately, after about a week's rest back home I recovered.

Some years previously, I had been told by the doctors that I had post-polio syndrome, brought on by ageing. This was an intractable disease, which could cause cold and numbness in the extremities, muscle weakness, and even respiratory distress, I was told.

The meetings went on, with Atilio taking my place, speaking to about 300 people.

News of my sudden return to Japan spread online, and about 500 people contacted *Le Monde*, but still, they wouldn't budge.

Receiving a decoration from Poland

In 2011, just after the Tōhoku earthquake, when we were all shaken by the scenes of devastation caused by the earthquake and tsunami in north-eastern Japan, the totally unexpected news came that the Polish President was to confer on me the Knight's Cross of the Order of Merit of the Republic of Poland for my contribution to the cause of Esperanto in Europe.

The following year, a symposium was held in the Polish parliament to commemorate the 125th anniversary of the birth of Esperanto, and I addressed the gathering in Esperanto as the guest of honour. I was given 20 minutes, including time for interpreting into Polish. I spent two days getting my speech to just ten minutes and practised reading it aloud a thousand times.

My hours of practice were rewarded when, after my speech, Senator and former Minister of Education Edmund Wittbrodt, Chairman of the Parliamentary Group Supporting Esperanto, shook my hand and said, 'Excellent!'

My friend, the Nobel laureate

When I was at the 2001 World Esperanto Congress in Zagreb, Croatia, Professor Selten from Germany struck up a conversation with me. He told me about the time in 1994 when he and his wife were returning home from the shops to find a large crowd of people outside their house. 'Has there been an accident?' they asked. 'Congratulations on winning the Nobel Prize!' came the reply. Apparently, the prize committee had tried to contact him by telephone half an hour before, but he had been out, so they went ahead and made the announcement anyway.

The professor, who was devoted to his wife and pushed her wheelchair for her everywhere, told me, 'The prize changed our life completely. Nearly every week I was invited to give a lecture in Cameroon, Rome, Poland or somewhere.'

He was awarded the prize for his work on game theory, which can be applied in decision making in such areas as management, government, and science. It is indispensable in computer science, apparently, although I have to admit it's all Greek to me.

We since met many times in different places and became good friends. In 2007, he came to Japan to deliver a lecture at Kagawa University during a severe storm. One thousand and seventy people braved the weather and listened with rapt attention to his speech, which he gave in Esperanto, admirably interpreted by Professor Shigeaki Nagamachi of Tokushima University.

After the lecture, a reception in honour of Professor Selten was held at the nearby Sanbonmatsu Royal Hotel, and a 22-member choir sang in Esperanto.

The next day I accompanied him to the Ōtsuka Museum of Art in the city of Naruto, not far away. This is an unusual museum, which houses a collection of ceramic reproductions of famous works from the world's great art galleries and museums. Professor Selten seemed very impressed with the collection, remarking that it would take years travelling around the world to see all the originals.

One God, one international language

In 1995, I joined a group visiting America to take part in the religious celebration marking the 50th anniversary of the founding of the United Nations, together with 56 others, including Kenshū Fujimitsu of the Tendai School of Buddhism, Seitarō Nakajima of Meiji Shrine and Kyotaro Deguchi of Oomoto.

A thousand members of religions from all over the world gathered together in New York. I introduced myself to Dean James Parks Morton of the Cathedral Church of St John the Divine, who was chairing the proceedings, and handed him an invitation to the following year's World Esperanto Congress in Prague.

In my invitation I had written, 'As well as the developing cooperation between world religions, I believe that an equitable international language is also needed for world peace. I would like you and Ms Morton to experience the world of Esperanto at next year's congress in Prague.'

The following spring, I still hadn't received a reply. Then, in May, when I had started to give up hope, the news came that they would be coming. That year's congress was attended by 3,000 Esperanto speakers from all over the world, and Dean and Ms Morton actively joined in the events. At the Oomoto sectional meeting, attended by 700 congress-goers, Dean Morton gave a speech.

In Prague with Dean and Ms Morton, Charles Rowe,
the translator of this book, and Ms Rowe, 1996

'In 1975, at the Cathedral of St John the Divine in New York, we departed from 2,000 years of Christian tradition, and invited Oomoto to perform a Japanese Shinto worship service at the high altar. This caused an uproar in Christian circles in America, with some people calling for me to be driven out of New York. But I believe in the ideal as taught by Oomoto, of "one God", with the religions of the world cooperating with one another; "one world", a world free from war; and "one international language", the equitable language for the world's people, Esperanto, which I believe holds the key to the realisation of world peace, and I shall hold true to this ideal as long as I live.'

All present were deeply moved to hear these words from Dean Morton.

Notable Esperanto speakers

Some interesting people have been counted among the speakers and supporters of Esperanto. These are some examples:

Ikki Kita (1883-1937, Japanese political thinker and activist). He proposed the use of Esperanto, maintaining that English would have the same poisonous effect on the Japanese people as the British Empire's export of opium had on the Chinese.

Inazō Nitobe (1862-1933, Japanese educator and diplomat). Nitobe believed that the world would be a happier place if people could exchange ideas in a common language.

Futabatei Shimei (1864-1909, Japanese novelist). His translation of Zamenhof's *Esperanto Reader* became a best-seller.

Romain Rolland (1866-1944, French author). Rolland said, 'If we learned to speak six national languages, our lives would be over by the time we had finished. But from the moment we learn Esperanto we are at the beginning of a new life. It's our weapon for the liberation of humankind.'

Erika Kobayashi (Photograph
courtesy of Tokyo Shimbun)

Josip Broz Tito (1892-1980, Yugoslav politician and leader of the Non-Aligned Movement). Famous for his slogan, 'Death to fascism, freedom to the people!' Tito also approved of Esperanto, saying, 'The major powers may push for the hegemony of their languages, but Esperanto is the truly international language.'

Leo Tolstoy (1828-1910, Russian writer.) 'After two hours' study, I was able to read and write in the language. Learning Esperanto will contribute to the creation of a Divine Kingdom on Earth.'

Charles Richet (1850-1935, French physiologist). 'Esperanto is as musical as Italian, as clear as French, and as perfect as Greek.'

Notable Japanese Esperanto speakers and figures attracted to Esperanto also include Asajirō Oka (zoologist), Kanji Ishiwara (army general), Hisashi Inoue (novelist), Tadao Umesao (anthropologist), Sakae Ōsugi (anarchist thinker), Sen Katayama (labour activist), Erika Kobayashi (author and manga artist), Toshihiko Sakai (socialist), Takamaru Sasaki (actor), Jinzaburō Takagi (physicist), Teru Hasegawa (anti-war campaigner), Katsuichi Honda (journalist), Kenji Miyazawa (poet), Kunio Yanagita (folklorist) and Sakuzō Yoshino (political scientist).

Other Esperanto speakers and supporters around the world have included Henri Barbusse (French novelist), Vasili Eroshenko (Russian poet), Zhou Enlai (Chinese premier), Ho Chi Minh (Vietnamese President), Ba Jin (Chinese novelist), Max Müller (German-British Indologist), Mao Zedong (Chinese Communist Party Chairman), Reinhard Selten (German economist) and Lu Xun (Chinese novelist).

Zamenhof, fighter for peace

Ophthalmologist Ludoviko Lazaro Zamenhof was born in 1859 in Białystok in present-day Poland, a city where he could hear Russian, Polish, German and Yiddish all spoken around him. Born a Jew, with a different language, customs, and religion from the other groups, he encountered interethnic conflict and violence arising from lack of understanding on a daily basis. Overcoming adversity and prejudice, he devoted his life to the creation of a neutral language that would allow people to converse freely on a basis of equality.

Brought up by his mother from childhood to believe that all people are siblings, Zamenhof made it his life's aim to bring about the understanding that, before we belong to any nation or tribe, we are first of all members of the human race. He went on to create a common international language in which anyone could freely converse with anyone else, while respecting the other's native language, culture, and religion.

Since the Middle Ages, there have been about 800 attempts at making a constructed language, but the only one that has survived is Esperanto, animated by its creator's lofty character and aspiration for world peace.

The 28 letters of the Esperanto alphabet are always pronounced the same. The accent falls on the last but one syllable of a word, without exception. There are no irregular verbs, and words can be built up using a regular system of prefixes and suffixes. The ability to create new words is built in, and although Esperanto has the one drawback that it is unrelated to languages from East Asia and Arabic, it can freely absorb vocabulary from other languages, including Japanese. For example, following the rule that nouns end in -o, *kabuki* becomes *kabuko*, *tatami* becomes *tatamo*, and so on.

By discarding redundant features, Zamenhof perfected a grammar that could be summarised in just 16 rules, taking up no more than two pages. Thanks to this streamlined grammar, it has been said that the language is five times easier to learn than English, ten times easier than Russian, and 20 times easier than Arabic.

At the present time, there are about a million Esperanto users in more than a hundred countries communicating with one another in various fields. Among languages using social networking services in international communication, Esperanto is said to come 15th out of 229 languages.

The world is now faced with the need to come together to respond to serious problems that perhaps even Zamenhof himself could not have foreseen. I can only hope that Esperanto will provide a ray of light to guide us through these troubled times.

The universe and life

I close with an extract from my favourite book *In Search of Meaning* by Hidemaru Deguchi.

The world is infinitely vast, and infinitely rich. What makes this vast world seem narrow and its riches seem poor is the human heart. This world can be a paradise, if only we can hold to an inclusive heart at one with heaven and earth, an open heart that neither chases after that which leaves, nor turns away that which comes to us. Rejecting the narrow self, let us adhere to the greater self.

Lift up your eyes and see the heavens.
Take in the mystery of the countless twinkling stars, the eternal brilliance of sun and moon.
Look down and behold the earth.
The trees spread their branches, the birds sing, the beasts multiply and people prosper.
The wind and the rain come at their appointed time; the seasons follow one another.
The sea dances, the wind makes music, the mountains change colour, the clouds play.
I am nurtured by the gods, by my parents,

Hidemaru Deguchi
(Photograph courtesy of Oomoto)

Lovers, friends and even those I don't know.
They are all working for me.
I could go on complaining all day.
A single leaf falling to the ground could irritate me,
The whine of a mosquito, the buzzing of a fly, the look on a person's
face, the weather.
All these things could drive me mad with anger.

From the atoms to the galaxies,
All heaven and earth are working unerringly,
Let us discard the narrow and the ugly,
And hold to the vast and the beautiful.
What gives us these things at the right time
Is what we call God,
What chooses from among them at the right time
Is us human beings.
Let us not lose sight of the infinite and the eternal,
Dazzled by the little things passing in front of our eyes.
Without rushing, at a relaxed pace,

Let us enjoy the beauty of the flowers
And the taste of the fruit of the trees
Within our hand's grasp, within walking distance.
Resting when tired, drinking when thirsty,
Moving by day and sleeping by night.
The way of nirvana is a smooth path.

The people of the world are all here with God's permission.
The enemy of one is the ally of another,
The foe of another is the friend of yet another.
All of us, are we not all God's children?
Let us forgive our enemies, let us give ourselves for each other.
Let us return, return to God's heart.

Oomoto's Esperanto activities began at Hidemaru's suggestion, nearly a hundred years ago.

Afterword

While writing this story, I frequently found myself going back in time to my childhood.

When I moved to the house where I live now, I was in the fifth year of elementary school. I was still in the same town, but our new house was on the outskirts, next to the sea. In this house, which used to be the home of one of my classmates, there were no proper *tatami* mats except at the New Year and the summer Bon festival; the rest of the year the family used rough straw mats. I was surprised when I saw this for the first time.

Carrying big baskets, as big as themselves, on their backs, my school friends cut grass to use as cattle feed. I was given a smaller basket, which I filled with plantain and dandelion to feed to the rabbits. We kept about six or seven rabbits in an apple box lined with straw. They used to call me by knocking on the floor with their hind legs. If we put males and females together, about a month later five or six young would be born. If we raised these up, we could get about ¥70 each for them, but I used to miss them after they had been exchanged for cash.

I have always been an animal lover. I often used to watch the oxen working in the fields. Not allowed to rest for a second, they worked until dark pulling the plough, gasping as they were chased around the field with a whip.

What was most distressing for me was to see a mother cow separated from its calf. Night after night, the cow would cry out, 'Give me back my calf.' Hearing the cow's wailing, I couldn't sleep.

When an animal could no longer work in the field, it would be sold for meat, and loaded onto a truck, resisting with all its strength. Often, missing its shed and its owner, an ox would escape and come running all the way back from the abattoir, tens of kilometres away.

I felt sorry for my classmates who had to work every day to fill their quota of one basketful of grass, but the suffering of the cattle broke my heart.

But as I progressed from childhood to youth, my distress at my polio became overwhelming, and took me to the depths of despair. Why wasn't I born normal? I even thought about dying. Then, my encounter with Oomoto showed me that all wasn't dark. To overcome my disability, I made it my life's task to do all I could to develop the Swany business, learning from all around me. Taking up this challenge was the start of my new life.

Reaching middle age, I developed a kidney ailment. By fasting and following a raw vegetable diet, I managed to fight off this disease, and somehow, I have managed to survive into my eighties.

I have also taken up the language problem, following Oomoto's teachings, and have made what efforts I could to contribute to the popularisation of Esperanto as an international language to take the place of English.

In every case, what lent power to my life was adversity. I learned, too, that fate does not deal a burden that is impossible to bear.

Holding firmly to Hidemaru Deguchi's teaching 'Be thankful for adversity, don't be dependent on others, take risks,' I have overcome various difficulties, and this I believe has helped me to achieve some degree of understanding.

I would like to thank my readers for their patience in reading my amateurish prose, and if any of it should be of any help, I could not be happier.

In writing this book, I have received advice from Oomoto Counsellor Kyotaro Deguchi, German teacher and President of the Kagawa Esperanto Association Kiyoyuki Kosaka, President of the Polio Association in Tokyo Mariko Koyama, former Executive Director Hiroyoshi Iwazawa and many other colleagues at Swany, my friends Tamotsu Nakagawa and Satoru Yamasaki, and my wife's friends Teruko Matsumoto and Minori Seyasu.

I was also helped enormously in preparing this book for publication by 'I', who wishes to remain anonymous. I would like to record my thanks to them, and to all the many others without whose generous help and support I could not have finished this book.

Etsuo Miyoshi, March 2021

著者紹介

三好鋭郎 （みよし・えつお）

株式会社スワニー相談役
1939 年、香川県に生まれる。生後 6 ヵ月で罹った小児麻痺の後遺症で、右足が不自由になる。
1964 年より、株式会社スワニーの後継者として、スキー・防寒用手袋のセールスに世界中を飛び回る。
ニューヨークで見たキャスター付きトランクを機内持ち込みサイズに小型化し、身体を支えながら運べる「スワニーバッグ」や、世界一小さく折りたためる車椅子「スワニーミニ」を考案し、ヒットさせた。
社長、会長を経て、現在は相談役。
株式会社スワニー
769-2795　香川県東かがわ市松原 981
URL http://www.swany.co.jp

不自由な足が世界を広げてくれた
―スワニーバッグ誕生物語―

〈検印省略〉

2022年 12 月 28 日　第 1 刷発行

著　者―――三好　鋭郎 （みよし・えつお）
発行者―――佐藤　和夫
発行所―――株式会社あさ出版
〒171-0022　東京都豊島区南池袋 2-9-9 第一池袋ホワイトビル 6F
電　話　03 (3983) 3225 (販売)
　　　　03 (3983) 3227 (編集)
F A X　03 (3983) 3226
U R L　http://www.asa21.com/
E-mail　info@asa21.com
振　替　00160-1-720619

note　　　http://note.com/asapublishing/
facebook　http://www.facebook.com/asapublishing
twitter　　http://twitter.com/asapublishing